Inviting ET

By Su Walker & Rev. White Otter

Illustrated by Su Walker

Thank you to all the experiencers who provided us with their personal CE5 stories. Your first steps in this new landscape help pave the way for others to follow.

Thank you to Karen Brown, whose first suggestions, writing and editing were invaluable to the beginning of this book.

A very deep thanks to Dodocat for all her creative help with the cover design and to Gavin for helping to get this book to press.

We give a very special thanks to the P'nti of the Sandia Mountain for initially contacting us, being such wonderful teachers and for all the things they have so freely shared with us.

This book is dedicated to all of our new friends here on Earth and across the galaxy.

Table of Contents

INTRODUCTION & FOREWORD

What's the Official Protocol for CE5 Events?

The first rule about planning a close encounter of the fifth kind (CE5) event is that there are no set rules, just guidelines from our own personal experience as to what has been tried and worked for us. No private official Earth protocol for extraterrestrial (ET) contact currently exists.

We do have quite a few details regarding telepathic contact that have been given to us by a Star Nation from Zeta Reticuli II, the P'nti. You will read some of what they have taught us, in their own words, scattered throughout this book. You can also learn a great deal about improving your own telepathic skills in the companion volume to this one, **The Telepathy 101 Primer** written by T'ni. It is a gift from the people of P'ntl to the people of Earth. If you would like a copy visit www.officialfirstcontact.com where you can download the primer for free. It is available in multiple languages. Physical hard copy books are also available.

If you and your event participants have not begun your telepathy practice in earnest, our Star Nation friends tell us it's an essential first step before you attempt your CE5 contact.

You, as CE5 event planners, along with your guests, are literally writing the rightminded Earth Human contact story as it happens. What follows are only suggestions toward a successful event. These are just some starting points, so don't limit yourself. Be creative. Your intent from the initial planning stages, to hosting the event, to following up with your fellow experiencers afterwards are ALL critically important to everyone's safety, as well as your success at ET contact. Events can be small or large or anywhere in-between, so not all suggestions here will apply to all events.

As you read this book do not let the lightheartedness nor the casual tone fool you.

This is very real!

BEFORE you decide you are going to host a gathering where you are asking for an extraterrestrial visit, we would like you to consider several really important things:

- You are not JUST asking to see an unidentified flying object (UFO) from afar.
- You are asking for an in-person visit from one of the many extraterrestrial nations who are already here on our planet (and they ARE here).

- You want them to come meet you in the flesh and talk. Remember, that means not just you personally but everyone else at your event as well.
- You, as the event organizer, are accepting the responsibility of keeping everyone at your gathering safe physically, emotionally and spiritually.

You and Earth Humans you invite to your CE5 are going to be facing a **lot** of new and scary things.

Even if everyone coming **wants to see** a UFO, even if they **want to meet** an extraterrestrial, we are here to tell you... **when it actually happens**, emotionally everything about your party changes dramatically, in an instant!

We want you to be as prepared as you can be. Know what you are walking into before you begin. Read this book from cover to cover before you decide not only IF you will host your ET invitational event, but also where, when, how and with whom you will put your close encounter of the fifth kind event together.

After your CE5 is a success and you witness things firsthand, your guests will need you to help them understand this big new thing they experienced.

Think through everything BEFORE you invite your first person. **CE5s are life changing events**; it will truly be something that you and they will never forget!

Do everything you can to have the best CE5 this planet has ever seen. Stay safe, have fun, learn, grow and have a very, very good time meeting your intergalactic relatives. They tell us they've been looking forward to this for a long time too.

-Su Walker, New Mexico (USA), June 2018

CHAPTER 1 - CE5 PRE-PLANNING

When we meet, a startle response is normal. Please see if you can put aside your fears and look us in the eye. Watch our body language. Feel your feelings. Listen to the thoughts in your head. You're not making them up if they don't sound like you because many of us are trained to communicate (with Earth Humans) and when you respond, then interaction can begin.

-T'ni from P'ntl, Sandia Station, New Mexico (USA)

There are a LOT of details to consider before you firmly decide that you are going to host your own close encounter of the fifth kind or CE5 event. Let's get started with all the things you need to think about.

Invite Who You Know

First, if you or any of your fellow CE5 party participants have experienced previous telepathic interactions, and participants *know* the nation or the specific individual they met or worked with, inviting that individual or group is a good idea. For instance, if one of your attendees has previous experience(s) with the P'nti from Zeta Reticuli II, invite that nation. If you are trying to reconnect with the nearby Sasquatch clan, send your telepathic message into the heart of their forest. (More about why we include the Big Brother Sasquatch Nations in this book later.) If it was visitors from one of the Pleiadian worlds, invite them.

Because telepathic connections were likely to have been established during that previous meeting, inviting a Star Nation that one of your participants has already met or interacted with will bring greater success.

Of course, inviting just anybody who happens to be flying by or telepathically listening on the night of the event can sometimes work, but you should not rely on this method for the best success.

The Exact Location, Time & Place

Try to decide exactly when and where your event will be several weeks or even months in advance, especially if you need to plan for nice weather. When you invite Star Nations, don't just tell them the name of your town, or invite them to meet you, "at the park." Instead, be as specific as you can. If attendees have a chance to look at the satellite perspective of your event location on Google Earth, they can see exactly how the property will look from the air. This will likely be your visiting nation's first birds-eye view as well.

We suggest all attendees know both the exact street address and the GPS (global positioning system) of the location as much in advance as possible. Your Star Nation visitors all have busy lives too and everyone appreciates a little planning ahead regarding consideration of both their schedules as well as yours.

Sending Your Telepathic Invitation

As soon as your CE5 event attendees know the date, place, time, and Star Nation(s) you are inviting, we suggest you all telepathically send up a personal invitation to that nation every day in some fashion beginning two weeks prior. If you have ten attendees at your event, and you all know a couple of weeks in advance, all ten of you (or as many as possible) need to telepathically send out a detailed, wonderfully imaginative, joyful invitation every day until the event is held! You want the ET visitors you are inviting to have time to put your gathering on their schedules. If during this stage any of the Earth Humans who send out their telepathic invitation get any kind of RSVP response back from a Star Nation before you gather, share it with the whole group so that everyone knows.

Quite a number of visitors to Earth are nocturnal. Because of this, CE5 organizers need to let attendees know if event hours will include staying up very late or even all night. Organizers will need to consider what to have participants bring and/or what accommodation is available on site for them.

Overnight or Not

Some groups choose to host their events completely outdoors at a facility where cabins and camping are available, and create a wonderful central bonfire that acts as a beacon that can be seen from the air. Others select a private home and keep their events smaller and more personal, preferring to view the night sky from a back yard or even large open garage door. Some events are all night or all weekend long while others gather just for the evening and stop at midnight or 2:00 AM. You determine which type of event works best for your group.

Private Homes & Local Parks

If you are hosting a smaller event in a private home, make sure you have enough parking. If you are planning on hosting your CE5 party outdoors at a local park, be aware of what time the park closes. Many facilities shut their doors to the public at 10:00 PM and some even lock their gates.

Get Permission

If you are hosting your event on private land, be sure to have a written, signed and dated permission slip from the land owner. Never ever try to conceal the fact that you are hosting an event designed to invite ET to come land on their property. Always be honest and upfront. Do you need liability insurance for your event? Can you even get it? If you ask, an insurance agent they may laugh at your question, and then offer you an event policy that covers everything from personal injury to the zombie apocalypse.

No Haunted Locations

We do NOT recommend holding your CE5 event at a haunted location or one with a potent emotional history like an old war battlefield or near a cemetery. The emotional residual energy of the area and/or the local ghostly residents would be likely to overwhelm the telepathic beginners in your group and you may end up with an event full of sobbing people. Save the "ghost busting" for another place and time.

Experts Among You

For large events, we designate a medical emergency person and a separate person to help handle any emotional crisis issues that may arise. We also recommend you have someone at your event or on your staff who is extremely experienced with the paranormal so that when those more advanced questions arise, you and your guests have an expert in your midst.

Meals vs. Snacks

Is your event going to be held long enough that you need to consider meals or just have participants bring snacks to share? Will you need breakfast in the morning? Will you provide hot water, tea or coffee all night long? Who will make it, care for the brewing, and take care of clean up?

Food Safety

No matter where you hold your event or how many people are coming, you will have a few health and safety considerations to deal with. If you are not hosting your get together in a private home with a proper kitchen and a refrigerator, how will you handle food preparation and storage? Be mindful if attendees bring dishes that spoil quickly. We've all had that one experience we remember from potluck dinners. If your gathering is more than half a dozen people, we recommend you assign volunteers to help with food setup, serving and clean up.

What Will Event Organizers Need?

Because organizers of any CE5 event are responsible for the physical, emotional and spiritual wellbeing of all participants, there are quite a few things to consider bringing to your get together. Large groups of 30 or more meeting at a rural location have different needs than smaller gatherings of half a dozen people camping out in someone's backyard. Strictly outdoor events will require you to bring more things from home than groups who gather at someone's house. You may or may not need all of the things we suggest, but if it's safety related in any way, we encourage you to think about it seriously. For the complete list of the things you really need to consider, no matter what size gathering you host, see Appendix I.

Electronics Anyone?

Can you bring cameras and recording equipment? Your group gets to decide whether they will be allowed or not. However, don't forget that it is NOT unusual for electronics to malfunction or have their batteries suddenly drained, usually at precisely the time you need to get the shot. Plan accordingly. Will there be a way for participants to charge cell phones? If not, make sure your attendees are aware of this fact. You may wish to consider using red light bulbs for ambient indoor or outdoor lighting. If you can operate and move around in a red-light environment, you won't ruin your night vision.

In my personal life, I've found having any experience from behind the lens of a camera often impedes upon the experience itself. Too often, many people concentrate on getting the "perfect shot" or "capturing the moment". Then they miss the moment itself. (And, from an Earth visitor's point of view, I'm sure a flashbulb in my face the moment I arrived on Earth would be as annoying as my driver license photo being taken without warning.)

-Karen, Florida, USA

Her point is well made. Don't miss the live action because you were looking at the world through the lens of a camera. However, in our investigations across the paranormal spectrum, we know there is a positive flip side to camera usage at CE5 events.

There are times when your camera or audio equipment can and does capture things your physical eyes and ears cannot see. Perhaps setting out several audio devices and placing a couple of cameras on tripods so they record everything, might be a worthwhile solution to examine.

Registration Stuff & Photographers

Those planning large gatherings may wish to consider if you will need to create registration materials, permission slips for photography, liability waiver forms, or any other handouts. Along with name tags or wrist bands, do you need to get large envelopes and prepare packets in advance for each participant? Do you need permission slips for photos to be taken of party goers?

Many events find that having a designated photographer, whose job it is to take photos of everything event-wise from start to finish, is extremely helpful. Some of those photographers get lucky and capture fabulous evidence in the course of doing their job.

Bonfire Anyone?

If your group is staying up all night, don't forget that the temperature will continue to drop until dawn. If you are planning a bonfire, you will need enough firewood for the duration of your event, fire starting supplies, a 5 gallon (20 liter) bucket of water or other water source, a long handled shovel or pitchfork, and a designated person who will be your fire tender. Fire tenders accept full responsibility for fire maintenance and safety the entire event start to finish, including cleanup and making sure the coals are completely cold before that person can leave. Once lit, you cannot leave your fire unattended. Your fire tender may need volunteer helpers to work in shifts.

Fun Stuff You Might Want to Bring

If a good portion of your event is being held outdoors, we encourage CE5 party attendees to bring blankets to place on the ground, or lounge chairs that can be moved into a reclining position for sky viewing. Encourage telescopes, binoculars, and monoculars. Recommend that attendees become familiar with prominent night sky constellations, individual star names and other astronomy terms. Apps are available for mobile devices, and you can purchase or print helpful materials, in order to identify stars in the sky.

It might be a good idea for everyone to learn to identify the difference between an airplane and an orbiting satellite. Share information with each other about standard aviation craft red, green and white lights and where they are usually located. If that dot of light you are watching in the sky moves unusually, point it out to everyone else and get their eyes on it too.

Should I have a "Do Not Bring" List?

Events should have some common-sense rules written out and made available to attendees at check in. However, there will be some rules that your guests will need to know prior to the event. Every event planner will create their own list of what attendees should not bring. Considerations include: alcohol, weapons, pets, children under 18, drugs, ouija boards, etc. Make sure whatever you choose on this "Do Not Bring" list is known ahead of time by those coming to your party. Here are some recommendations based on our experiences.

Drinks Anyone?

Should you include alcohol at your event? We do not recommend it. You are all going to be practicing telepathy during your CE5 gathering and you want to be able to gain control over your growing skill set, not inhibit or lose it. Remember, your attendees may be facing some pretty powerful fear issues and it's better to have them in control of their faculties. We've put in our two cents. The choice is up to your group.

What About Bringing Pets?

Should you include your pets in the party? Pet participation will depend entirely on the pet. If your pet is easily agitated or appears nervous, you may opt to keep them in another room or leave them at home. Some animals will cause absolutely no problems and can even alert you to the presence of visitors. For larger events, however, we recommend leaving your pets at home. Service animals only.

Can Kids Come?

Should you include children at your CE5 event? Honestly, at this stage we do not recommend the event for anyone under legal age. Parents, regardless of how much you think your child might be ready, you yourself have to experience a close encounter of the fifth kind before you can even come close to making this decision for a child. You must know that you can handle your own self first! Leave the kids at home.

No Ouija Boards Please

While there are many simple board games that can work to help people practice their telepathy, there is one we do not want your participants to bring. Ouija boards are not toys. A Ouija board is not "a game" and it most certainly is not for beginners! We DO NOT EVER endorse the use of a Ouija or spirit board as a beginner's tool in telepathy practice. Too many things can go wrong. It is a powerful tool that does work *but requires advanced training*! If your beginner students try to bring them for use, we recommend they be put out of sight or removed from the location.

What Do Earth Human Attendees Need to Bring?

What should you consider having participants bring to your ET meet and greet? Every event will have a different list for what they suggest their attendees bring in terms of:

- General supplies
- Food/beverages
- Equipment, phone, chargers and batteries
- Clothing, medicines & toiletries
- Bedding & chairs

We have created a general all-purpose list to get you started with ideas for your event attendees that you can copy and revise. See Appendix II.

Just to let you all know, if you come to a CE5 event we are hosting, expect to be told to leave your cell phones in your vehicle. I personally think the damn things take your attention away from the really important stuff. Use your eyes, use your ears, reach out with all your senses. YOU have apps your cell phone will never have, use 'em!

-Rev. White Otter, New Mexico (USA)

What if Nothing Happens?!

What do you do at your CE5 event if nothing happens, no ships show up, no unusual things occur, and there's no sighting of an extraterrestrial? What if halfway through the night it begins to thunder and lightning, then downpour? Won't all your CE5 event attendees be disappointed?

Well sure, they will be disappointed. There is never a guarantee that even if you do everything right, that you all will experience a CE5, ever, period. Honestly, those are the chances you, your staff and your attendees all take. From the moment they decide they would like to attend your event, everyone must have this understanding.

Remind folks when they sign up for your CE5 party and again at the beginning of your event of the fact that the ETs may not show up. Remind them there is no guarantee of a seeing a ship, experiencing the laws of physics being bent, or being visited by a person who does not call our world, or our dimension, home. Disappointment is understandable but can be moderated by everything else that your people can gain from deciding to try proactive contact. Set the intention at the beginning of your event that there is a still a lot to be gained from your CE5 gathering, even if the ETs don't make it.

So, what do you do with all your attendees if you get rained out or if things are in any way disappointing? You talk! You learn from each other's experiences. You practice your telepathy with each other and hopefully see some improvement in your skills. You get a chance to find your tribe, the people who understand and accept you for who you are, strange experiences, weird interests and all. You have fun! You meet people!

Make sure you make back up plans in case the weather turns bad for any reason. If rain chases you all indoors or into tents, you want to have things that everyone can still do.

All your hopeful CE5 attendees will naturally have some frustration if nothing happens, or if your event is a wash, but that doesn't mean the party was a waste of people's time. Even if the ETs do not show up, do everything you can to help folks have a great event and still say at the end, "Let's get together again and try this one more time."

We hope this isn't the case for you. We hope you will have great success at your CE5 event. The bottom line is to be aware you are trying to create a rightminded event to introduce Earth Human people to Star Nation people and vice versa. Put yourself in their shoes. If you were a visitor meeting we Earth Humans for the first time, how would *you* want to be invited to *your* first meet and greet? Your CE5 event participants, Star Nation as well as Earth Human, are all practicing new skills and overcoming their anxiety of the unknown. Don't forget, Star Nation people coming to see you have fears too. Try to be patient and understanding of *everyone's* emotions whether you have Star Nation visitors or not. Be gracious. Do what you can to put *everyone* at ease at your event, whether they are Earth Human or from somewhere else.

Why does life exist?
Because consciousness seeks a beautiful expression.
Why does telepathy exist?
Because consciousness seeks to share its life.
                    -T'ni from P'ntl, Sandia Station, New Mexico (USA)

Official First Contact isn't about tech.
It's about emotions...
Both yours and ours!
                    -Tlkm from P'ntl, Sandia Station, New Mexico (USA)

CHAPTER 2 - LET'S GET THIS PARTY STARTED!

Housekeeping

At the beginning of your CE5 party, all attendees need to know a few standard things. Where are the bathrooms? Where is there fresh water to drink? Who should they go to for emergencies? Introduce your staff and fill any volunteer work duty slots that are open at the beginning of your event to help keep things running smoothly.

Be Mindful of Your Thoughts

Remind everyone to please be mindful of their word choice and use more socially correct language. You know all those bad words you are not supposed to say on television? You don't want to be offensive nor do you want to accidentally teach a trainee or visitor from somewhere else in the galaxy inappropriate language! As we approach Official First Contact, our Star Nation friends tell us in-person visits will become more common and that there will be a lot more visiting telepathic nations on Earth from all over the galaxy. Please be mindful of your words and thoughts.

While we are on the subject of language, we would like to remind everyone to never refer to a Star Nation person or being as an *alien*, a *grey* or an "it." That would be rude. You are speaking of people who are sentient beings. Use the words "he," "she" and "they" please. Remember, you are trying to be welcoming, not insulting!

> *Please don't call me "a grey!"*
> *I don't call you a pink or a brown.*
> -*Tlkm from P'ntl, Sandia Station, New Mexico (USA)*

We do understand why you are inclined to use terms such as alien and greys. Only limited information has been available to the general public for a long time, and these terms are used by the media. Many older articles about extraterrestrials use these blanket, generic terms because they did not have any better information at the time of writing.

However, we are in new times. More information is readily available about our Star Nation cousins than there has ever been before! We must usher in this change, so that we can also help teach others the correct terminology and noun/pronoun use.

You want a CE5, right? A close encounter of the fifth kind with extraterrestrials? If you're going to step into their realm, you have to play by their rules.

-Rev. White Otter, New Mexico (USA)

Experiencers and Contactees, Not Abductees

Some of your participants may have previous Star Nation experiences where they were taken on board a craft or removed to another location and returned. The term we most commonly hear used by and for these individuals is "abductees."

The whole idea behind holding your CE5 event is to not only meet but speak with folks who are not from here. Your party participants are not victims, they are proactively seeking interaction and understanding. Because of this, we encourage all of our participants to permanently drop the word "abductee" and instead use "experiencer" or "contactee" when referring to themselves.

The CE5 Buddy System

For larger events we recommend establishing the CE5 Buddy System. Every attendee gets assigned a buddy (fellow attendee) whom they keep an eye on physically, emotionally and spiritually. Any time you have a total of 10 or more participants and staff, we recommend doing this. Make sure you count *everyone* at the start of your event. You need to know exactly how many people are under your care.

CE1 through CE5

We talk about a CE5 being a close encounter of the fifth kind, but what is it really? Dr. J. Allen Hynek, a consultant for the US Air Force developed what's known as The Hynek Scale. Many people refer to it as the Close Encounters Scale.

- CE1 - I saw a light in the sky: You have a visual sighting of an unidentified flying object from afar.
- CE2 - Something affected a person or the environment: A UFO event where a physical effect is alleged: electronic or vehicle malfunction, animals reacting, physical paralysis, physical traces on the ground affecting nearby plants, a chemical or radiation trace, etc.
- CE3 - I saw a person or a being: UFO encounters in which an animated creature is present whether its humanoid, a robot, or another type of being.

- CE4 - Something trippy happens: Your sense of reality is transformed in some way. This includes absurd, hallucinatory or dreamlike events.
- CE5 - Voluntary back and forth communication with a Star Nation person: A UFO event that involves direct communication between Star Nation people and Earth humans.

Introductions

If your group participants are new to each other, make name tags available and schedule some time to have your guests introduce themselves. We encourage our attendees to think of a funny story they would share with a Star Nation visitor about their life, and tell that to the group as a possible introductory exercise. Remember, your extraterrestrial cousins are just people too, and they come here because they want to learn about Earth, you, and your life experiences. They frequently laugh at the same silly things we do.

Things To Do At Your Gathering

So now that you understand more what a CE5 is, what kind of things can you do at your ET pajama party? First, knowing that everyone in your group is familiar with the basics of rightminded telepathic protocol is key. Star Nations tell us they like many of the same things we do in a social gathering. They are very attracted to conversations with emotionally honest, mature, loving people. The also tell us food, music and dancing are universal appeals; so are joy and laughter. Visiting nations are looking for Earth Humans who have conquered their fears and are *really* ready to meet their galactic cousins.

The night of your event, when everyone first gets together, you will want to have a few planned activity ideas. Practice your telepathy with each other. Play games that might further your skills. Don't be afraid to play music, dance, sing, joke and have fun. You can break off into smaller groups if desired.

Come up with a fun group exercise that telepathically tells your invited Star Nation...

"We are all here, come on down and join the party!"

Welcoming the Invisible Man

We find it's easiest to treat your Star Nation visitors as you would any Earth Human visitor, although in the beginning we admit can be a little tougher if you can't see them directly. Plan on immediately discarding any discomfort you have speaking out loud into "thin air." When you speak telepathically, you can also speak out loud simultaneously. As an

Earth Human you are used to communicating verbally so just add the telepathic sending to your spoken words. Have some fun practicing. It might feel a little awkward at first, but you'll get used to it.

Should you designate a few special chairs for your Star Nation guests? Well, you don't want them to stand with no place to sit do you? If you sense anyone, should you set out food for them? You would offer it to other guests that came to your event, wouldn't you? So, the answer is yes!

We understand you don't know the visiting nation's dietary restrictions, but you certainly can try offering natural foods from your area. We suggest organic fruits and vegetables as good choices, but honestly several of the Star Nations have confessed to liking things like chocolate, coconut cream pie and pizza, so you'll have to make some decisions.

Items ETs Can Handle

Put some items out that can be examined by your Star Nation visitors. These can be the same items you used in the telepathic exercises. Tell your off-world guests they are free to look at these things and explain their everyday use and/or their sentimental value. If you get the opportunity, you can try asking any perceived visitors to pick up or move an item...they might even do it.

Here Comes the Telepathy Fun

Activities at your CE5 event could include social games that further your telepathy such as cards, dominoes or any short game that is easy to learn. Agree ahead of time it's okay to use telepathy in some good-natured cheating. You might try playing charades or other social games that seem appropriate for the size of your group. More about important role playing that we encourage you to do in a bit.

Be sure you plan some music time. This can include dancing, karaoke, musical jam sessions... use your imagination. The idea is to create joy!

Across the galaxy...across species, cultures, spiritual beliefs, space, time and dimensions...music, rhythm and movement inspire all of us!
-Tlkm from P'ntl, Sandia Station, New Mexico (USA)

It's Not a Competition

Some of your CE5 event attendees will be further along in their telepathic practice than others. You need to be careful to not make your gathering into a "who is best at telepathy" contest. Those in their first year of practice will find it useful to talk to those with more experience and you want to create a fun, encouraging atmosphere, not a competitive one.

Talk Around It

Sometimes it's not easy to put words to what you are picking up telepathically. Remember your goal is ultimately to be able to *fully* describe something accurately, not just put a word or name to an incoming perception. *You will often* receive a blend of information all at the same time... sights, sounds, smells, sensations, emotions, distance, direction, and time can all be combined in one telepathic message. We tell students to "talk around" what you are receiving if it is difficult to describe directly.

No Matter Your Language

When you receive telepathic input, it will always be interpreted in your brain by your own primary language centers. You will hear your telepathy in your native tongue. If two of you receive the same telepathic message at the same time, but you speak English and the other person speaks French, each of you will receive the message accurately, but in your own language.

What's a Ping and What Does It Feel Like?

A ping is our term for sending or receiving a telepathic communication of any kind. "I'm going to ping you tomorrow at noon" means "I'm going to send you a telepathic message tomorrow at noon."

How do you know if someone is pinging you? Again, sharing experiences among your attendees will help everyone learn. Here's our list to get you started:

- Usually a sudden background thought of a specific person springs into your mind (behind your foreground thoughts), seemingly "out of nowhere".
- You may feel a physical response, from an itchy nose to goosebumps.
- You may recognize a friendly greeting feeling, a "hello", a touch or kiss, etc.
- You may suddenly stop what you are doing to instinctively hush the noise around you as if you need to "listen" for something.
- You may have a sudden urge to get in touch with someone via phone or other means. You may not be able to get a person out of your mind.

As you practice telepathy, you ARE going to run into some very unusual things. It comes with the territory. Get used to it. Expect the laws of physics to be bent... and not just little!

-Rev. White Otter, New Mexico (USA)

Physical Reactions to Pinging

We say "the body knows first" when it comes to you getting pinged by another person. Often your physical body will respond before your mind recognizes, "Oh, I just got a ping." These physical responses can include:

Eye movement: Are you suddenly moving your eyes back and forth as if trying to read or comprehend something? Looking to the left helps access information intuitively. According to Neuro Linguistic Programming, looking left and up triggers visual processing, left and horizontally triggers auditory processing, and left and down triggers kinesthetic processing. Looking horizontally from left and right helps to trigger past-to-future connections. If you get pinged, it is not unusual to find your eyes moving as if trying to "read" information. When you hit on a truth or accurate piece of information, your eyes will suddenly stop scanning left and right and stare for a moment. If there is more information to be had, you may feel a nudge to resume your back-and-forth eye movements because there is more to glean.

Other common body responses include:

- Gut feelings, tingling hands or other body parts, butterflies in the tummy.
- Nostrils flaring or an itchy nose.
- Suddenly very hot or cold hands.
- A funny taste sensation.
- Goose bump or nape of the neck hair response.
- Reaction in the forehead/third eye area.

Always, always pay attention to your very *FIRST* perceptions...even if you don't understand them fully at that moment. Be okay saying, "I'm not sure I understand what I got, but this is *what* I got." (Translation, I don't know if I fully understand everything I perceived telepathically, but this is what it was in as much detail as I can describe.)

Improving your telepathy doesn't happen in a day or a week, or even a month...but after just a hundred days of practice, some of our students are now receiving regular visits from us.

-T'ni from P'ntl, Sandia Station, New Mexico (USA)

What is it NOT?

Sometimes, when trying to put what you are perceiving into words, it is easier to say what something is not. You can simplify your telepathic search by eliminating whatever you can, instead of directly searching for what it is. What details can you eliminate telepathically? Can you say what it isn't?

Thinking in 3D and Pinging on an XYZ Axis

Remember to ping on an XYZ axis. Someone may be at a higher or lower elevation than you. Don't forget to ping in 360 degrees! This is especially helpful when attempting to locate a pilot in a ship flying overhead. It is also useful in search and rescue missions at locations with varying topography.

We look for those who have done a thorough internal look at themselves. This type of deep self-examination is performed by very few. Finding folks who fully own up to their past actions is a rarity. We delight in those who have emotionally "done the dark look."
- T'ni from P'ntl, Sandia Station, New Mexico (USA)

Some people freak out when they see our ships.
They don't stop to think there might be people inside.
Some people freak out when they see what we look like.
They don't stop to think there might be a person inside.
Some people freak out if I speak to them.
They think they're going crazy!
They don't stop to listen to my words.
If I speak to you, will you listen to my words?
Will you answer? Or will you freak out too?
-T'ni from P'ntl, Sandia Station, New Mexico (USA)

CHAPTER 3 - WHAT IFS & FACING FEARS

Many of your CE5 attendees will have never seen a craft up close, witnessed a portal opening, or met a visitor to Earth before. They are coming to your event because they want that chance. However, everyone will still have fears that need to be addressed.

Adrenaline Spikes and Sudden Overwhelm

We need to talk about how to handle the adrenaline, fears and overwhelm that may arise within your group. Remember, as the organizer, you are not the only individual at your meet ET event who's going to be afraid. You will have your own fears and issues to deal with; *those* you probably have some inkling about. However, you will *also* have to deal with everyone else's at the same time and you probably don't have any idea what kind of past fears they could be bringing to the party. Some of the people attending your CE5 gathering may have had frightening previous Star Nation or UFO experiences prior to coming to your event. They may have to face these old fears all over again.

Everyone's reaction to a sudden burst of adrenaline is different. The effects of this kind of hormone spike can run the gamut. People can get shaky and light headed, hyperventilate, panic, or just plain fall down in a cold faint! Some Earth Humans become hyperactive, get suddenly protective, or go into warrior defensive mode. A few folks just plain want to run away as fast as their little legs can carry them.

You will ALL be facing your own fear/adrenaline responses. It's critical that all event goers understand they need to help one another to stay calm and deal with everyone's fears rightmindedly and appropriately. Remember, if the person next to you is trembling, on the edge of panic, or if you yourself feel that way, we teach our students that sometimes it helps to simply hold hands. We also teach students to verbally remind each other, "You're okay. You're really okay," to encourage them to self calm.

"It Ain't Nuthin' But A Thing"

There are times where you have to, emotionally and physically, keep yourself together while at the same time the person next to you is struggling to hold back their panic. Back in the 1960s White Otter learned a phrase that helped him cope with some horrendous situations during the Vietnam War. When he and his outfit had to help each other stay calm either during or after a traumatic event, they looked each other in the eye and repeated, "It ain't nuthin' but a thing."

"Ain't nuthin' but a thing" is a way of putting off your emotions. It's a defensive wall designed to remove some of the traumatic extremes temporarily. It doesn't erase the emotions, but buys you a little more time to pick and choose *when* you can deal with shocking situations later. It doesn't speak to the issues that stun your psyche and your physical body, but it does help compartmentalize them so that they can be dealt with at a more opportune time.

"...or not. Be warned. That's where the insanity comes in, the "or not" part of dealing with it. It will stay with you all until you DO deal with it."
                                                            -Rev. White Otter, New Mexico (USA)

Getting Gobsmacked

When you get smacked in the face with anything that bends the laws of physics and destroys your sense of reality, we don't know if PTSD (post-traumatic stress disorder) is exactly the right terminology. It's an extreme emotional shock to your values and morals of understanding that's for sure. You can call it psychic thrombosis, PTSD, or getting gobsmacked... it doesn't matter. It's all the same stuff.

Yep, It's Real

When the laws of physics get tossed on their ear right in front of you, the key to overcoming your own personal reality shock it is to first admit it's really happening. After "one of those experiences," if the shock, fears and trauma aren't dealt with and end up getting buried in your psyche, they become an unhealed wound.

Those kinds festering emotional wounds only can be healed through divulgence to another party. In our experience, this is key. You gotta talk to somebody who understands! That's why we tell you to "go find your tribe," to form these emotional companionships and trusted bonds so when the need arises, all you have to do is reach out.
Remember, you're only as sick as your secrets.
                                                            -Rev. White Otter, New Mexico (USA)

If Someone Wants to Leave

If someone wants to leave your event unexpectedly due to their fears, then they are telling you they are not ready for a CE5 experience. Let them leave. Encourage them to keep practicing their telepathy, working through whatever their issues are and to stay in contact with you after the event. There's no rush, give them their own processing time to work through their own emotions and fears.

Shifting Away from Fear: Su's Story

How did I shift from being terrified and unable to sleep because of my past experiences with ET, to no longer being afraid? When my conscious encounters first started twenty years ago, in the beginning I was completely freaked out! That summer when my ET experiences suddenly became very real, I had to figure out how to deal with my fears all by myself. It wasn't easy,

I had not just one but two different Star Nations unexpectedly wake me up in the middle of the night first by a "tall white" individual, and two weeks later by a group of four Zetas.

In mid-June of '98, sometime after midnight, I was in bed and had been sleeping soundly, but I snapped awake when I realized someone very strange was in my room. As I watched, a very tall, creamy white individual who obviously was not from Earth walked up to the foot of my bed. Adrenaline pumping, I sat straight up in bed and yelled at him, demanding to know what he was doing in my room! When I did so, this tall ET with large dark eyes got a totally shocked look on his face and then turned and bolted straight through the wall. That scared me!

Ten days later, it happened again. This time when I suddenly awoke, four, short, strange looking individuals with large heads and dark eyes were standing at the foot of my bed. One held a device in his hand that he had touched my lower leg with. Then, as abruptly as I had come to, instead of yelling at this group, I remember thinking I had to return to sleep... with all four of them still standing there. That scared me even more!

I saw these people with my own eyes and I knew I was not dreaming. But because I had no one to talk to about it and no way to process what had happened, I went through this horrible insomnia for nearly forty-five days. Every night when I tried to go to sleep, the memories of my visitors would return and so would the racing thoughts of the unknown. For six weeks I laid awake in bed afraid to shut my eyes and drop off. My fears told me that if I closed my eyes they might come back.

I had thousands of questions! Would they return? What did they do with the device they had? Would they take me somewhere? What would they do to me? Would I vanish into the cosmos never to be seen again?

And what if I didn't see them again? What if that was it and they were never coming back? What if I never learned who they were or why they visited me? What if I never got any answers? The not knowing... that was the hardest part for me to deal with. I wanted to understand what the hell had happened to me and why. Who were these guys and what did they want?!

Finally, after struggling with the overwhelm for more than a month, very late one night, exhausted and in my pajamas, I walked out into the darkness of my back yard and began yelling angrily at the sky at 2 o'clock in the morning.

"I don't want to be afraid anymore! I JUST want to understand! Would you PLEASE tell me who you are and what you want! I want to remember! I want to help you, but I can't if this is just one sided! Please, treat me the way you want to be treated. Please JUST TALK TO ME!!!"

As I was screaming at the stars, crying out my frustrations to anyone who might be listening, pleading when something big shifted inside me.

I suddenly realized that if I looked at the actions and the intent of these strange looking peoples who had suddenly appeared in my bedroom, they were not trying to scare me. In fact, when I really thought about it, they seemed to be doing everything they could so that I wouldn't be afraid.

I abruptly stopped yelling at the night sky and stood there in my pajamas having an apostrophe (epiphany) moment.

Even though no dialog had taken place, their intentions seemed to be rightminded. When I looked back over everything in detail I could tell that they were doing what they could so that I wouldn't be afraid of them.

Why would they do that?

Why would they bother?

Then it hit me. If they didn't want me to be scared, that meant that in some way they cared about my feelings and my wellbeing. They CARED! They cared about me the same way I would care if the roles were reversed. If they cared, then just maybe there was a possibility for real communication. I had no idea if or when that might happen. I remember taking a deep breath right there under the moon and purposefully calming myself. I suddenly realized that I didn't have to choose to be scared.

I looked up at the stars for the first time in a month and a half with hope. My fears weren't completely gone, but now they were under my control. With one last backward glance at the moon, I went back into the house, up to bed, and was able to go to sleep for the first time in weeks without the fear and with a new understanding and hope.

-Su Walker, New Mexico (USA)

Ill Effects

Can any of your event people develop a headache, lightheadedness or nausea after a really super strong telepathic encounter? They can, and this idea alone can create some issues when people approach a potential contact experience. Luckily, you can assure your people that we usually see these ill effects in folks who approach Star Nations in a wrongminded fashion, not a rightminded one.

If any of your participants do develop symptoms, your designated medical person needs to be prepared. If symptoms become extreme, seek professional medical advice immediately. Do we honestly expect problems like this to happen at your CE5 event? No probably not, but it's always better to be ready.

So how *do* you face all these potential things? What do you do with all the unknown fears everyone else at your "ET meet and greet" has?

Sharing Contactee Stories

When you've never done something before, hearing other people's first-hand stories and experiences helps alleviate people's fears more than you know. Often one of the most powerful and important things you can do at your CE5 event is to give people time to talk with each other and retell their own personal stories of previous ET or UFO contact. We highly recommend adding it to your party's list of important things to do.

Meet ET - Discussion and Role Play

When you know you will be facing something emotionally or physically challenging, it helps to both talk and walk through it several times first. We *highly* encourage all attendees to either discuss what they would do or role play meeting various Star Nations for the first time.

Because CE5s deal with so many unknowns, it helps to present your participants with several scenarios so that everyone has a chance to think through, impromptu style, what they would do and how they would act if a UFO or an ET suddenly showed up.

These exercises can be both hilarious and profound at the same time and give all your attendees the chance to come up with a spontaneous rightminded reaction to an unknown scenario. It also gives them the chance to critique each other and add suggestions.

Feel free to research actual CE5 contact stories and then use your imagination to come up with your own what ifs and role-playing scenarios that help your guests deal with their fears of the strange and unknown.

If you are planning on roleplaying with props, see Appendix V for ideas. If you would rather just talk through possible unknown situations as you're watching the night sky, the following will help get your "what if" discussions started.

The first thing we teach trainees here at the Sandia Station is our basic mission protocol.
   Cause no fear.
   Do no harm.
   Leave no trace.
                          -Tlkm from P'ntl, Sandia Station, New Mexico (USA)

Zetas Among You

We know from talking with our friends from Zeta Reticuli II that they have a "cause no fear, do no harm, leave no trace mission protocol." We also know they have the capability of remaining cloaked or invisible and that, while they normally do not speak, we have experienced them making other sounds, moving things, and in general being very curious.

The P'nti tell us that ground missions where they visit us at our homes are seldom done solo. Where there's one Zeta, there's usually more. They tell us missions usually range from 2-6 people.

What do our P'nti friends tell us about their ships? They describe their vessels are "extruded" coming out as one seamless oval, cylinder or classic saucer shape, often metallic silver or pure white with no seams.

Use the following "what ifs" to spur discussion:

- What if you see a white oval craft zip in low and hover over your group?
- What if someone in your group spots that "shimmer effect" movement of a short, cloaked someone circling your event participants?
- What if an attendee has a raspberry blown in their ear from an unseen individual less than a foot away?

What will you do? Who will grab the recording equipment? Will you send out a telepathic greeting? Should you pull up an extra chair for any perceived cloaked visitors? What will you do or say next?

Equipment Failure

Contactees and researchers of UFO phenomena may be familiar with the subject of suddenly battery drain or equipment malfunction, often precisely when a ship or individual shows up. We find the phenomena SO common in fact we honestly recommend participants just plan for it.

- What if your new batteries all suddenly drain and your flashlights won't work?
- What if your equipment turns itself on or off?
- What if your equipment records something your eyes don't see and your ears don't pick up?

Do you review your footage or assume you may have a visitor close by? Should you ask them if you can try to take their picture (again)?

Cold Spots, EMF Spikes & Hair Raising Effects

We remind CE5 event goers to pay attention when the hair begins to rise on the back of their arms or the temperature unexpectedly drops in a localized area. Something or someone is causing it!

Electromagnetic frequency (EMF) spikes, sudden silence, cold spots and your physical body reactions are all common occurrences during CE5s. We tell our event participants, only slightly tongue in cheek, that "the body knows first... sometimes the brain catches up."

- What if everything becomes eerily quiet, the hair on your head begins to stand straight up?
- What if the electromagnetic frequency (EMF) suddenly goes off the charts in a localized area?
- What if you experience a localized extreme temperature drop?

If you suddenly become cold, do you grab a jacket and keep it to yourself, or tell the group? Do you nudge the person next to you and say, "I've got goosebumps, do you?" Do you grab the EMF meter to find out where the electromagnetic reading is strongest? What do these changes mean?

Approached by Strange Humans

CE5s don't always involve witnessing a ship coming down from the sky. They also don't always involve strange looking ETs.

Sometimes a Star Nation, who looks JUST like you or me will approach your event on foot (from a vehicle, the street, the woods) and you don't think anything of it until you start observing these unexpected visitors in greater detail. While it's not a hard and fast rule, often SOMETHING about them will be a little off.

- Is their speech modern and use of slang current?
- Is their clothing odd in some fashion?
- Are they wearing clothing or footwear of unusual construction?
- Do they launch into strange questions with no introduction?
- Do they know private things about you they shouldn't?
- Is their body language automatic and natural?
- Do they portray themselves as a person one of your event participants knew in the past?

Talk through unexpected "Earth Human" visitor possibilities with your attendees.

- What if an "Earth Human" couple unexpectedly exits the nearby woods and approaches your group at 3 AM?

- What if "the park ranger" walks up out of nowhere and just stands at the edge of your group, observing your event but remains completely motionless and says nothing when you greet him/her?
- What if "a New York City cab" suddenly pulls up with two "normal looking" people... but it's midnight and your event isn't anywhere near NYC?

Do you treat your unexpected visitors like weirdos and shoo them away, or do you realize something isn't adding up? Will you invite these strangers to sit and talk and offer them something to eat? Will you remember to ask if you can record them?

Portals and Event Horizons

No matter if you witness them suddenly manifest in the sky or on the ground, whenever you see a doorway of any kind unexpectedly show up, it gets the old adrenaline pumping!

We teach participants to treat any portal or event horizon with the same protocol you would treat a ship that comes down to land. Do not approach, attempt to touch, or go through the doorway. You don't know where it leads and you don't have enough information to know if it's physically safe for you to be anywhere near it.

- What if a ship suddenly manifests from a swirling vortex of clouds that have suddenly formed over top of you?
- What if a ground circle 3 feet (1 meter) across forms just 10 feet (3 meters) from the chairs you and your event participants are sitting in?
- What if you are inside a building and you see the main wall suddenly dissolve into a sea of strange colored lights?

What steps will you take, in what order? Given the size of the portal, do you expect a vehicle or an individual to come through it?

Sweet and Innocent Animals

We have personally experienced extraterrestrials trying to portray themselves as animals we either know well or our ET visitors thought we would not be scared of. Telepathic nations can pluck an image from your own mind and instead of you seeing the ET and their real physical body, they may implant an image of something like a super-sized sweet and innocent bunny instead. (Which may or may not have huge black almond shaped eyes and telepathically talk to you to try to convince you it's really a bunny.)

We have heard reports of various extraterrestrial nations portraying themselves as tall owls, squirrels and rabbits. Our own experience was a four-foot tall telepathic shark that stood up on its tail.

In another of our CE5s, while camping in southwest Wisconsin (USA) August 5, 1999, we also personally witnessed an "Earth animal" (in our case a large grey squirrel with dark almond eyes) slowly, gently float down out of a clear night sky from a great height and land on the ground just meters away, and look at us expectantly as if to say, "What? I'm a regular grey squirrel from Earth. Don't you believe me?".

Normally, squirrels just don't do that.

- What if you a "really big owl" with unusually large eyes begins observing your event and keeps creeping closer and closer, acting very unowl-like?
- What if you sneeze and the rabbit munching on the grass nearby says, "Bless you!" telepathically inside your head?

What's your response and then what do you do?

Gravity Shifts

During one close encounter at our home in the fall of 2013, we experienced a sudden loss and reestablishment of gravity while sitting in our own living room. It came with approximately 20 minutes of missing time.

We are also aware of being "dropped" back into bed and bouncing slightly as we impact the mattress on numerous occasions. (That bounce will get you every time.)

- What if a gravity wave suddenly passes through the area?
- What if you unexpectedly experience a few moments of weightlessness?

How will you and everyone deal with it?

Sasquatch

Many readers interested in requesting a CE5 from a Star Nation wonder why we talk about the Sasquatch in our *Inviting ET* book. The reason is simple. The P'nti have informed us that not all the Sasquatch Nations are necessary from Earth and that you can find these peoples on other worlds. Theirs is a body type that is extremely durable and has the ability to withstand many harsh environments.

We understand from the P'nti that many of the Big Brother Sasquatch are also telepathic. The same protocols for inviting ET work for requesting interaction with the Big Brother Bigfoot Nations as well. Many CE5 events held outdoors in remote areas are often surrounded by forest and you may indeed attract interest from a nearby Sasquatch clan as you send up your telepathic greetings.

- What if you witness a full-size tree suddenly shaking violently all by itself with no visible cause?

- What if you see yellow or red glowing eyes peering out at you from the nearby trees?
- What if a tree knocks, whistles or a tremendous roar comes from the nearby forest?
- What if a pebble, tossed from the woods by an unknown individual, lands at your feet?

Will you recognize these actions as typical Big Brother behaviors? Will you greet them warmly and gift them with food?

Clothing Issues

On several occasions, we have experienced inexplicable clothing changes that make us aware we have had a missing time event. What do we mean?

If you suddenly realize your clothes are somehow not on your body the same way you remember getting dressed, you may want to think twice before you chalk it up to an excuse like, "I must have been tired when put my clothes on."

Whether they are inside out, on backwards, fastened wrong or if you oddly find yourself in clothing that isn't your own, consider whether or not you can account for your entire day or night, as the case may be.

Those who've had a "close encounter of the medical checkup kind" can imagine how, if an extraterrestrial was running late and hurriedly helped you get re-dressed and back home again after a visit to their ship, they might not know how you normally put everything back on.

- What if you wake up and find yourself wearing everything inside out and backwards?
- What if you "just go for a little walk" but when you return you realize your shoes are now on the wrong feet?

What are your next steps?

Strange Stickiness & Getting Dipped

After some CE5 events, we have occasionally found our skin seems to be slightly tacky or sticky. Once in a great while, we also experience an unusual tan or amber liquid suddenly draining out of our ears. These same experiences have also been described by other contactees. Over the past four years, several individuals who have talked to us about their missing time encounters describe waking up at home in a bathtub of cold water or coming to in the shower with the water running. None of them remember entering the bathroom much less turning on the tap.

So what's going on here?

The P'nti of the Sandia Mountain tell us that some Star Nation visits can include what they call "wellness checks." They tell us that some experiencers are occasionally "dipped" in a nutrient solution to improve their immune systems or take care of pathogens. The stickiness on the skin and the amber liquid in the ears can both be indications of this "dip" process. Those experiencers who wake up in their bathtubs and showers are there because whoever the ET was who returned the contactee to their home realized that some residue was still remaining that needed to be washed off.

- What if you wake up tomorrow, discover a strange amber spot on your bed pillow and also realize your skin has a very slightly sticky feel?

How will you handle it?

Invisible ETs

Some of your Star Nation visitors may show up but maintain invisibility as their mission protocol. Teach your participants that cloaked individuals cannot be easily seen by looking directly at them, but they can be viewed more easily using peripheral vision, angled reflection, or full spectrum cameras.

How do you know if there is an invisible someone in your midst? We describe invisibility as "looking at a heat shimmer." There is a wavy quality to the air around a person or thing that is cloaked that you can often pick up during movement.

- What if one of you spots the tell-tale signs of an invisible person circling your group? Will you invite them over and try to get them to interact with you?

You can have all kinds of fun with this type of what if scenario discussion and role play at your CE5 gathering. Use your imagination. We encourage you to look over the ET role playing exercises in Appendix V.

Putting attendees through exercises like these has proven to be extremely helpful in getting your CE5 party guests to not only think through what they would do and say in various possible scenarios, but they might physically act it out as well.

CHAPTER 4 - WILL THE LAWS OF PHYSICS GET BENT?

Can you expect to witness the laws of physics to be bent at your event? Honestly... maybe. What can *that* kind of experience be like? We don't mean a scenario such as, "Oh my, I just saw that 'star' flash brightly and disappear. It must be a UFO!" No, we're talking a little more than that.

Between Rev. White Otter and myself, we together possess more than 65 years of personal "I was there and yes it really happened" paranormal and ET experience. We've seen more Star Nations and witnessed more craft now than we can count.

What have we personally experienced in our own close encounters? Here's the list of just a few of the things we have seen that bend the laws of physics more than just a little:

- Moving balls of light of all sizes and colors or bright flashes where no known light source exists.
- Auditory noises and voices spoken by an invisible someone. This can include laughter, whistles, whispers, and raspberries blown in your ear so close you have to wipe away a little spittle.
- Unexplained dampening of sound or complete sudden silence in a localized area.
- Sudden EMF spikes or static electrical charge on everyone and everything.
- Camera or cell phone batteries draining suddenly without explanation.
- Lights and/or equipment turning itself on or off, or settings changed in front of your eyes.
- Sudden unexplained gusts of wind that seem to be under intelligent direction, lightning strikes, or blasts of heat or cold. Individual objects that are extremely hot or cold for no apparent reason.
- Shimmering invisible outlines of people moving around our home, some of which you can only catch in your peripheral vision or angled mirror reflection.
- Large, undulating bright balls of plasma-like energy that move under intelligent control. Plasma that manifests into a sentient being in front of you.
- Extremely loud mechanical sounds or vibrations that fill the air but have no known source.
- Bilocation of objects or people. Observing objects or people vanish or appear.

- Sudden, unexplained changes of clothing, whether someone's shirt is suddenly on backwards and inside out, or two people inexplicably are wearing each other's attire.
- Plants or animals that appear to telepathically talk and have distinct personalities.
- Forest animals that look as if they are made of iridescent blue light.
- Animals floating down from the night sky and gently landing on the ground nearby.
- Clouds forming images in direct response to telepathic communication.
- Intelligent beings visually manifesting in and speaking from water and smoke.
- Telepathic communication that appears to come from water, fire, earth and air and clouds.
- Small spherical balls of fire flames with no visible energy source, rolling along the ground, moving under intelligent control.
- "Earth animals" of unusual size or who possess large dark eyes and who speak or behave strangely.
- HUGE invisible walls of energy that completely stop you in your tracks or bring you to your knees.
- Time distortion; either stretched or compressed time, completely missing or lost time. Arriving too fast to a destination and not being able to explain the reason for non-use of gas and arriving several hours early given the distance driven (without speeding.) Time looping and repeating.
- Gravity vanishing and re-establishing. Gravity changes to one object or person only.
- Star Nation visitors moving through solid walls.
- Star Nation visitors who appears to alter their perceived shape and appearance into a completely different species and back again.
- Earth aircraft becoming invisible, or suddenly visible as if "out of thin air".
- Vessels which enter or exit through dimensional openings, portals or tunnels they create and control in the sky.
- Beings who enter or exit through dimensional openings, portals or tunnels they create and control on the ground.

The list goes on, but you get the idea. If you witness something strange or unusual at your ET meet and greet, let others know! Tay appention (pay attention), stay alert and be ready to say, without the fear, "Now THAT was interesting!"

The Laws of Physics Were Bent: Kevin's Story

My name is Kevin Estrella and I live in Ontario, Canada. I have had various close encounter and CE5 experiences going back as far as I consciously remember to the year 2000. To date I have had four craft sightings, missing time, clairvoyance, telepathic communication in the form of other's thoughts, telepathic visual images, pings, and synchronicities (weekly now, they are a normal part of life when you are tapped in.) I have had visitations to my home and have met with Star Nation beings. Sometimes, I have gone with them in their ship, all voluntarily. This is now becoming a regular occurrence. But have I ever been afraid? The answer is YES.

One of my biggest contacts with a UFO occurred August 21, 2014, 10:30pm when an interdimensional craft flew across my backyard 100 yards (90 meters) from me. It was a beautiful disc, orange/red in colour and glowing like hot coals. It appeared seconds after I stepped onto my deck, like it was waiting for me. It displayed weird physical properties such as being 2 dimensional (had height and width, no depth), it was surrounded in a field of plasma. As I watched it move away, the craft appeared to be opening some kind of white, swirling vortex/portal in front of it as it left.

I was just dumbfounded. I had waited for a UFO sighting my entire life but what I witnessed, I was not prepared for! For two weeks after the experience I was shaken to my core. My paradigms of reality were BROKEN. I kept replaying the event over and over in my mind trying to grasp in my infantile understanding of physics how to put it into a framework I was familiar with. Was it a military craft? Nothing seemed to fit. My mind kept trying to make sense of it from what I know here on Earth, but it was a futile effort. I couldn't do it. The laws of physics had been bent!

-Kevin Estrella, Ontario (Canada)

Perk Up Your Ears

Don't forget to notice what your ears are picking up. Listen to *all* the actual sounds around you. This is especially important at night in rural areas. If you are next to the forest, you may hear unusual sounds coming from there. If you are in an area where Sasquatch reside, because they are also considered a telepathic nation (along with other woodben of various sizes) Big Brother could be drawn to your event just to check it out. If you know they have been reported in your area, stay alert to strange noises, glowing amber or red eye shine or voices coming from the woods.

Listen for Specific Responses

While we didn't get to "see" our visitors directly at our CE5, we were aware of their presence! They played drums on the wall. Someone thumped a metal can in response to a joke. Someone even knocked on the piano bench moments after I got up from playing... just two feet from where I had moved to.

- Karen, Florida (USA)

Knock Knock Who's There: Jack's Story

I was one of the three Twitter friends who attended the first ever "ET pajama party" in January of 2018. That first night, the three of us were still just getting to know one another and it wasn't very much after dark when I started to notice what might be multiple presences around me. Not long afterwards, all three of us witnessed strange unexplained knocking on both the outside and inside walls of the home. We immediately investigated but came up with no logical explanation.

As the hours went by, we did all kinds of fun telepathy stuff. I got so that if I paid attention, I could track the movements and position of something at the edges of my peripheral vision. The invisible slight shimmer would move across the room and I was able to track it visually and sometimes audibly.

That night, I also had my first really solid telepathic successes with another person. During our telepathy games, I could clearly feel when specific telepathic signals were directed at me. I was even able to pick up details sent to me in an image that I didn't expect coming. Boy, when I got the confirmation on how specific I could pick things up telepathically, it surprised me but also really helped!

Not once during the entire CE5 event did I feel scared, threatened, or like something bad was going to happen. The crew of ETs that showed up had a good sense of humor and seemed to have a good time interacting with us. My most enjoyable moment was when it sounded like they were, honest to God. tap dancing. I found that funny. Without a doubt that night we had real CE5 stuff going on. I'd do it again in a heartbeat.

- Jack, Kentucky (USA)

Sudden Eerie Silence

Also, listen for a sudden absence of sound. If the entire area goes instantly silent, and the crickets stop chirping and the birds stop singing, alert *everyone at your gathering* to stop what they're are doing and instantly go completely silent too!

Tell all your staff and attendees that if this happens to freeze and open up every sense they've got! *Pay very close attention to everything that's happening at that moment.*

Utter silence at night outdoors in nature does not happen for no good reason. Something or someone caused all of the natural world around you to shut down simultaneously. Is the silence caused by an Earth concern... did a bear just come out of the forest or is it something else? Did your invited guests arrive?

"Hello the Clouds!"

We also remind participants to pay attention to the clouds overhead because most all extraterrestrial craft can generate cloud camouflage for cover. They can also shape clouds into anything they wish. If you think there might be a ship anywhere overhead, the P'nti have taught us the standard telepathic greeting from the ground to the sky that all that Star Nations understand is, "Hello the clouds!" Even if there are no clouds in the sky, this is still the standard phrasing to the local skyspace.

UFO Roman Candle: Jack's Contact Story

If you're like me, sometimes you feel a little crazy for believing that all this ET stuff is real. You doubt yourself, or at least I did. I had to have undeniable proof that couldn't be messed with. One night I decided to go outside and test the stuff I was reading in the Telepathy 101 Primer *to see if it was real or just make believe crap. I was going to ask for a sign.*

I trudged outside beyond the light of our farmhouse to the back of the property one night in late March of 2018. I'd been studying the primer for maybe 100 days or so by that time. It was cold and I walked the fenceline for a while before I stopped, looked up, and sent out a telepathic greeting like they teach. I didn't even speak it vocally. I just took a deep breath and tried to picture my thoughts traveling up toward the stars.

"Hello the Clouds," I telepathically called out.

The response came instantly!!!

Suddenly, from somewhere beyond the fence, just into the wooded treeline, a UFO lit up the entire area like a fireball and shot vertically straight up from the forest. It looked like a giant Roman candle, but there was no sound, just this bright burst. In a split second it had gone from the tops of the old oaks to a speck in the night sky before it vanished completely.

My jaw hung open. They responded the very instant I sent the request out! I hadn't said one thing out loud, not one! The fact the entire request and response had been telepathic made a believer out of me. I don't know how long I stood there shaking my head before I started to chuckle.

"Well okay then!" I said with a grin and laughed again. "Telepathy works.... who knew."

- Jack, Kentucky (USA)

Blink Blink

Will you see your visitors physically? Well, that depends. Most Star Nations don't have any issue with blinking at you from a position high above your event in their ships. We tell event participants that when they telepathically send up a greeting to also ask any ET pilot that can hear them to please double blink their ship's lights. The unofficial nickname for this request is "blink blink."

Photographing ET

The P'nti have told us that their Star Nation official protocol does not technically allow them to be visible or pose for photographs or video prior to Official First Contact. (Sorry, no selfies just yet.) However, we Earth Humans are clever and have found a few work arounds.

While you might successfully detect movement in your peripheral vision, we also suggest setting up a large mirror where participants can catch images in angled reflection in your main event room or outdoor location. Sometimes, catching images in the right angle of mirror reflection allows for clear glimpses of visitors (we do not exactly know why.) The P'nti have also informed us that full spectrum cameras work much better than night vision ones.

Strange Smells

In addition, we need to say something about noticeable local changes in smell. Some Star Nations have a pleasant floral scent, or no detectable smell at all, while others, such as some of the Sasquatch nations do not quite have the same hygiene habits we enjoy in our culture. Some visiting nations may come with a *strong* odor. We do mean strong too; think of wet dog rolled in ripe poo and you would be pretty close. Please don't say anything negative to make them feel unwelcome. Alert your fellow CE5 participants that you may have a visitor... just don't forget to say hello when you can breathe again.

Colored Lights

At least one Star Nation who identify themselves as originating from the area of the Pleiades is known for a change in light spectrum when they arrive, and have a faint medium blue glow around their physical bodies. Others arrive following a sudden burst of white light. Some multi-dimensional nations first show up in a spherical orb (white or colored) manifestation. Speak with these orbs just the same way you would if an individual were standing there instead.

Giggles, Snorts, Whispers and Whistles

Another fun little-known side note about our friends from Zeta Reticuli II. The P'nti, even though they do not normally speak out loud, are rumored to giggle and snort when the laughter is flowing. Whispering or whistling might also occur, so be alert! Any mouth sound you can make that does not involve vocal chords, they can too. If you hear such a noise with no known source, tay appention.

The Cloud Winked Back: Su's Story

Rev. White Otter and I were returning home from a trip to southern New Mexico in early May of 2016. I was in the passenger seat, enjoying the desert scenery when I glanced up at the sky and noticed a distinct eye forming in the patchy cumulus clouds off to my right. Over the course of two or three minutes, the single eye turned into two, and a P'nti face formed.

I was surprised and delighted. "Well hello there!" I thought to the cloud face. "That's a delightful image. My compliments to the artist."

To my utter surprise, a moment later the cloud face turned toward me, its eyes directly locking with mine for several seconds. Then, in a slow, leisurely fashion, the cloud face formed a large cumulus smile and then unexpectedly, winked at me!

First my jaw dropped open and then a large grin spread across my face. I couldn't believe what had just happened. I started to laugh. I had been taught about UFO pilots being able to form clouds around their craft, but this took what I have come to call "cloud camouflage artistry" to an entirely different level! Just another confirmation that telepathy works!

- Su Walker, New Mexico (USA)

During first contact missions, we are often as nervous as you are.
Let's all be kind when we meet, please.
-Tlkm from P'ntl, Sandia Station, New Mexico (USA)

CHAPTER 5 - THEY'RE HERE! WHAT NOW?

How do you know when your Star Nation guests have arrived at your event? Well, it's different for everyone. Don't just rely on your eyesight! Use ALL your senses. Don't forget the *Telepathy 101 Primer* instructions of trusting your peripheral vision. Also, rely on your intuition! (Telepathy works, who knew, right?) You might feel a change in the energy around you. Your ears may start ringing. You might pick up your visitors telepathically. Be alert to all kinds of subtle changes because honestly, you do not know what to expect. Every CE5 experience is completely unique!

Cultural Norms

While many telepathic connections feel light and gentle, we do know that some Star Nation's initial telepathic contact can also be sudden and extremely (but unintentionally) loud or strong. This kind of powerful contact can happen to only one individual in the group, or the message may be received by everyone. It can be a startling experience, or even frightening, in spite of the fact that you may be inviting it, expecting it and hoping for some kind of contact.

At the very beginning of your event, please help all your event participants understand that there are many Star Nations who visit Earth, and you can't expect them all to completely understand all Earth's cultural norms. If we are truly honest with ourselves, even *we Earth people* don't know all the thousands of details about every culture on Earth either... and it's OUR planet! In that respect, we are very much alike.

Please treat any telepathic or personal contact as if it is a learning situation for you as well as your Star Nation visitor(s). If anyone in your group gets a contact that is far too loud, politely speak up and ask if they would please telepathically communicate with a little softer volume. If they are too close to you, in a nice way let them know what a comfortable distance away is for you. We suggest using an arm's length. If their natural power or emotional intensity is overwhelming, ask them to please be much softer or easier with you, as you are just a telepathic beginner.

It's possible they were shouting really loudly because, telepathically, people at your event were inadvertently shouting when attempting to communicate with them. Perhaps in their exuberance, your group was sending telepathy too strongly and your invited guests thought this higher volume and more intense manner of contact was normal for you.

You just don't know. Understanding one another through open and honest communication is important. You can't assume anything!

Don't Bug Them, Be Gracious

By the way, we recommend during first meetings that you never pester any ET visitors about their technology as if their possessions and knowledge are more important than who they are as people. Make friends first... tech talk can come later.

Remember, your event is also a training ground for ETs to address their own fears of contacting you. Help all your guests think through how they themselves can personally be gracious to each other as well as anyone not from Earth that might be stopping by.

Sometimes They Just Show Up

Star Nation individuals have also been known to just appear at events seemingly "out of nowhere." Occasionally strangers, who appear to be Earth Human (often a couple), emerge on foot from the nearby area (street, woods, vehicle) and just walk straight up to you or another participant and begin conversing. It has been reported that these individuals will often launch into unusual topics with little introduction.

If, at your event, you suddenly have people who look like you but who are dressed a little oddly, who speak differently, or who behave in a manner that tells you they may not be from anyplace local, don't automatically dismiss them as weirdos! Offer them a seat, a beverage and food and see what they have to say. Ask if you can record them. You never, ever know what to expect or how you will be visited.

Should you touch, offer to shake hands with or hug an ET or multi-dimensional being? ONLY if you ask and they tell you it's okay. Remember that everyone has his or her own personal space; respect everyone's boundaries.

Being Startled is Completely Normal

So, what DO you do if a ship lands or an extraterrestrial being suddenly shows up standing next to you and says "Hi!" First, being startled is completely normal. Instruct all your attendees to use their powers of discernment even if they themselves are still trembling. *Any* CE5, no matter if it's your first or fifth one, is a *big deal* and your body is allowed an adrenaline response. No matter what you do to prepare, the adrenaline response <u>will</u> come. However, we want all participants to decide ahead of time to do everything they can to change their adrenaline flight response (wanting to run) into a proactive positive assertive reaction that helps them stand their ground and work through their fears. This is why we highly encourage the "Meet ET" role playing!

We tell all our participants, if you witness a ship up close or a Star Nation person in the flesh, take a big gulp of air, stand your ground and LOOK really hard at the entire situation. Take in every detail you can. Open wide every sense you have and use your discernment. Keep your gestures and your eye contact non-threatening. These are your guests arriving.

Fear is just a fight or flight reaction; simply biological, nothing more. Once you put that initial 'Whoa!' reaction aside, you can let your heart rate slow back down to normal and then take the time to think and feel it all out. I did go through a period of upset and fear. But this is a strange and wonderful universe full of other possibilities. I eventually embraced the fact that there is so much that we do not understand, and finally came to accept that what I saw just was.

- Kevin Estrella, Ontario (Canada)

Laser Pointers are a No No

If you've spotted a UFO and that ship's pilot has "blink blinked" their ship's lights at you, feel free to work together with your group's flashlights and blink blink right back. Remember, their pilots like our pilots have eyes; whatever you do, don't shine any laser pointers in the direction of a UFO and blind somebody accidentally.

It's So Small! Is It A Drone?

Sometimes, instead of a craft that carries occupants, you'll be visited by a small drone. These are usually spherical and can range in size from 10 feet (3 meters) to about the size of a basketball. We never assume we know for sure one way or another whether we are dealing with just an unoccupied drone or not. Remember, even if a craft is no larger than a basketball, it can still have a pilot... don't assume.

X Marks The Spot

If a craft flies in really close, your group can use several of your flashlights to indicate where there might be a good place to land. How do you do that? Believe it or not, the P'nti tell us X marks the spot is fairly universally understood. If you have spare flashlights, lay out the lights on the ground so their beams form a giant X as large as you can make it and then send up your brightest "Hello! We've marked a landing spot for you if you care to come meet in person." If they respond and approach, make sure everyone stands as far back from the area as you can. We suggest a minimum of 100 giant steps.

What If A Ship DOES Land?

If you and your group witness a ship landing, stay together and stay back. Unlike scenes in the movies, landing procedures and disembarking can take time. Pull up a chair and have a seat. Keep your eyes open for several things. Are there other ships close by? Do you witness any other air traffic of any kind? (Unmarked helicopters have been known to suddenly show up.) Is someone recording the event? Everyone is sure to have more than a little adrenaline running through their veins so you might want to have your video equipment on a tripod to eliminate a shaky piece of footage.

Do We Approach?

Always, always wait for the vessel's occupants to emerge and approach you. It could be that you'll see a door open and a visitor to Earth step out. It could be they will emerge in a transport vehicle. It could also be that they will just suddenly show up in your midst. Be ready for anything.

Even if the ship lands and an entire hour has gone by and no one appears to have emerged, do not approach the craft. Instead send out a telepathic welcome again and see if you anyone in your group gets a solid response.

If you wish, you may also demonstrate welcome by setting out a ring of chairs that can be easily seen and indicate with both telepathy and gestures, "Honored guests, please come sit with us and be welcome."

Stay alert and use your peripheral vision. Remember, sometimes you don't honestly know if they are standing right next to you unless they *want* you to know.

What If A Ground Level Portal Opens Up?

Don't let the New Age sounding word "portal" throw you. Just say door, it's easier.

If some kind of a door opens up at the ground level, to be honest you don't have enough information to know exactly what you're dealing with:

- You don't know if a ship has landed and remained invisible, but you caught the light spill effect when they opened their doors.
- You don't know if you're seeing an opening to another dimension or another time.

- You don't know if the door is actually an event horizon that leads to somewhere else here on Earth or some distant region of space.

Because you don't know, if you see a door of any kind opening, keep a healthy distance and use the same protocols you would if a ship had just landed at your event.

Orbs are People Too?

Along with other experiencers, we have witnessed orbs of various colors that move under intelligent control. Sometimes they appear by themselves and vanish as quickly as they came and other times they dance around the area inspecting things before taking off. We have also spoken with several folks who report telepathic contact with these balls of light. Occasionally, contactees report orbs that suddenly flash and a moment later a person is standing in its place. We don't know exactly how to classify these experiences or precisely what all these sightings are. We suspect we are witnessing more than one kind of phenomenon that somehow gets lumped into a catch all category people are calling "orbs." We recommend you treat them as intelligent with the possibility it may be a scout of some kind.

Where There's One...

Our friends from Zeta Reticuli II tell us it is unusual for their missions here on Earth to be solo ones. Usually the P'nti travel in pairs or groups of six or less. If someone at your event spots a single Star Nation person, make sure you automatically start looking for others.

When You See Somebody...Immediately Assess!

If you witness an unusual looking person of any kind, *do not approach them.* Let them come to you! Observe your visitors non-verbal body language. Stretch out your feelings telepathically and gently ping them with a greeting of welcome. Does the very first impression you receive back from that new visitor feel rightminded or wrongminded?

What If They Feel Wrongminded?

First, let's deal with the less likely scenario. What do you do if your CE5 contact feels wrongminded? What if you hear a deep growl or witness a dark shadow being approach your group. What do you do next?

We teach everyone just because something or someone displays the absence of light, like a dark mass or fog, do not assume it is evil or demonic in nature. Dark does not automatically mean evil. Dark means you have no light reaching your eyes from the person or the thing usually because they're using the energy for something else. Dark all by itself should be considered neutral as far as a threat to you or your event goers are concerned. So, if a "shadow person" shows up, does that automatically mean they are evil? No, it does not, not unless their words, intentions or actions tell you otherwise. Have we seen shadow people be positive, neutral or negative? We have had experience with all of the above. You cannot assume.

In August 2013, Su and I were outside standing together in the narrow breezeway between her home and garage back in Iowa. It was about 10 o'clock at night and suddenly, a full-sized shadow person, complete with arms, legs, body and head, forms less than 5 feet from us. In the light of the streetlamp, it approached, passing within inches of us both. Our jaws dropped and we looked at each other in the partial darkness as if to say "Are you seeing this too?" The shadow being then walked over to a bench about ten feet away, sat down, and formed into a partially see through man, dressed in Ojibwe clothing from approximately 200 years ago. He seemed very polite and sat, just looking at us for several minutes before simply fading away. Was he really Ojibwe? Was he really an ET who plucked a memory from Su or me and portrayed himself that way? I don't know if we'll ever figure this one out.

-Rev. White Otter, New Mexico (USA)

If you hear a growl, should you react as if it's a threat? It's true, it might be a threat, but then again it might not. You better pay attention and *immediately* discern everything you can about the situation! However, it completely depends on the growl. If the growl is combined with a deep or gravelly voice and sounds in any way like language, you might react entirely differently than if the sound truly feels threatening and menacing. What does *the entire* situation tell you?

There's Safety in Numbers

If something or someone wrongminded shows up at your event, we teach that there is safety in numbers and to immediately but safely move your group en masse away from the danger. If any of your participants spots a potential threat, or feels threatened in any way, always err on the side of caution. Immediately alert everyone, band together as a group and move to safety! It doesn't matter if a black bear comes up out of the woods, a skunk waddles toward you from a nearby field, or a strange looking someone emerges from a dimensional portal that just feels bad.

The best recourse you have for your group in situations that feel dangerous, threatening or wrongminded in any way is to quickly and quietly exit to a location of safety, count noses so you make sure everyone is present and accounted for, and then reassess what your next steps are going to be.

We cannot guarantee any individual from any Star Nation will always be good or always be bad. Individuals are individuals. But if you have one bad individual from a Star Nation please just do not dismiss that entire nation. You would not wish us to do that to you.
-T'ni from P'ntl, Sandia Station, New Mexico (USA)

What If Our Telepathy Isn't Working?

Could you be dealing with a robot, android or data gathering drone? Maybe they speak out loud like Earth Humans do. If telepathy doesn't appear to be working, default to using gentle gestures and words.

Meeting the Rightminded

If you believe your visitors to be rightminded, very slowly and gently use positive gestures along with your telepathic and verbal greetings. Don't everybody in your group speak at once. Elect a spokesperson please to be your primary contact, or if your group is small, take turns. Have that elected individual greet them with welcoming thoughts, words and gestures. Observe their reactions. Do they keep their distance? Do *they* approach? Do everything you can to show them and treat them just as you would any invited honored guest(s) whose language and customs you are unsure of. If you think and act rightmindedly, you have every chance of a positive interaction and exchange.

Greeting Gestures

The P'nti have told us that greetings vary widely among Star Nations. If the visiting nation has claws, shoving your hand toward them to shake can be considered a threatening gesture. We teach our students the greeting gestures they have taught us:

First slowly show them your open hands. Then gently bring your palms together over your chest with your fingertips up, and nod your head or bow slightly. You may also form your hands together in a empty bowl, and "offer the bowl" in their direction. This is the universal gesture of, "Welcome, I have something for you." You may also take the bowl of your hands and gesture toward an empty chair indicating non-verbally, "Please be welcome and come sit with us."

What If Their Bodies Aren't Like Ours?

While we are learning more and more everyday about the various Star Nations that visit our planet, we recommend all participants just assume any visitors they see will NOT look like Earth Humans. We do not even assume they will be bipedal. They may not have two arms, two legs and one head and walk on two solid feet.

I met a water-being once. I don't know where it came from, it was suddenly just there. This was in 1970 and I was in Vietnam on night patrol. I swear, it looked like a person, and had a place for eyes, nose mouth just like me... but it was made of moving fluid like clear water. I could kinda see through it. Then, as fast as it came, it was suddenly gone. Weirdest damn thing I ever saw.

-Rev. White Otter, New Mexico (USA)

I was only 17 when I met somebody that didn't have a body like you or me. I remember it being warm outside, mid-summer and around 11 or 11:30 at night. A person sized, slow moving, undulating blob of iridescent golden plasma approached me. It actually floated right up to me and telepathically spoke! Normally I would have totally freaked out, but he was so kind and gentle. We spoke for hours and he ended up teaching me many things. Even now, forty years later, I can still recall all the details. It was that powerful of an experience.

- Su Walker, New Mexico (USA)

CHAPTER 6 - MISSING TIME

Will you or your participants experience missing time at your event? It's not a given but honestly, yes, you ALL could. It is entirely possible.

What is missing time anyway and why does it happen? Okay, let's just call it what it is. We are really talking about telepathic mind control where another person manipulates not only how you can act, but what you are allowed to remember.

When a contactee tells you they had missing time, what they are really saying is for an unknown period, they were controlled by someone or something else that also made it really hard for them to retrieve any memory of the gap of missing time in question.

When a person has missing time, <u>their memories aren't gone</u>. Those memories are still in the experiencer's head. It simply comes down to the fact that the original events were stored in a dream state and you must re-enter that same slower brain wave state to retrieve them. The memories may surface on their own given time spent in alpha. However, if you really want to get at them faster, seek out a competent hypnotherapist and have them assist you.

It's Like A Bad Movie Edit - Kevin's Missing Time

I had an experience of missing time with my first conscious UFO sighting. We were swimming in a lake up in Huntsville, Ontario late one night. When suddenly we heard a sound above us like a firecracker fuse. I look up to see a huge object as bright and circular as the full moon, but it was coming straight for us right above our heads. I could tell its trajectory because there were flames shooting from behind the perimeter. It was only 1000 feet (300 meters) above us when all of a sudden there was a FLASH! I am still staring upwards, but now at a quiet, starlight night sky.

It would be many years later when I was being questioned in a radio interview about my experiences, and the host said, "People we have spoken to who have experienced missing time, describe it like being a bad movie edit." When they said that, the hairs on my arm stood up because that is exactly what I experienced! All my life I wanted a UFO sighting, I look up to finally see one, and then the DVD remote forward button was hit and the climax skipped. Worst movie edit ever! I want my money back!"

- Kevin Estrella, Ontario (Canada)

Cause No Fear, Do No Harm, Leave No Trace

Why do Star Nations manipulate your memories and actions in the first place? Because most Star Nations visiting Earth operate on a protocol of "cause no fear, do no harm, leave no trace." They don't want you to be scared and hurt yourself or something or someone else. It is part of their standard operating procedure. This much we've been told by the P'nti.

So, your attendees all need to understand this kind of thing is possible and they have to be okay with the idea that someone else can shut them down. That's a pretty big pill to swallow if you think about it. They don't know if or when it might happen but accept that it's all part of the risk of choosing to purposefully seek extraterrestrial contact.

Folks who attend your event looking for a CE5 become willing to take the chance because for them, the potential for contact and subsequent dialogues that can follow are _that important!_

The CE5 Buddy System Revisited

Because of this, and especially for groups over ten people, we highly suggest you develop a CE5 event buddy system so that no one goes anywhere alone. Your buddy is to know where you are at all times and vice versa. If your buddy starts talking or acting unusual or strange, alert your designated emotional support person immediately. If medically something seems amiss with your buddy, tell your medical person right away. _Never leave anyone alone for any reason if they are behaving unusually._

The Gesture for Missing Time

We teach all participants that the emergency gesture for "lost or missing time" is to urgently tap two fingers on your wrist where you would normally wear a watch, as if demanding, "What time is it?!" Some people, when they first come out of missing time event, can have limited verbal skills and find talking difficult. It is not unusual for them to seem like they are walking in a dream, but they can often still gesture and write or draw easier than they can speak. If at your CE5 event, anyone comes up to you unable to talk in full sentences, but they are urgently tapping their wrist with two fingers, that person is telling you they **just had** a close encounter of the trippy kind and they need your help right now!

What should you do if you or any of your event participants suddenly discover they are missing time, or believe they had an intense encounter during your CE5 gathering?

Make them Sit Down and Stay Put

If a participant alerts anyone at your gathering they _just experienced_ a missing time event, or know they just came back from an encounter, stop everything you are doing. Get that experiencer to sit down to avoid any potential of falling down. While many "lost time" experiencers truly are perfectly okay post encounter, you just want to make sure.

Be aware that they may currently be, or may quickly become agitated, disoriented or confused. They just went through a BIG deal and it can sometimes cause a shock to people emotionally and physically that they don't see coming. It's the symptoms of real physical shock we want you to watch for. They may exhibit nausea, dizziness and vomiting. Never leave a person who has just experienced missing time alone or out of sight if they have reported their encounter at your event. Even if they insist they are okay keep your eye on them. We've witnessed people go from "I'm fine" to a combination of fear, panic and extreme emotional overwhelm in a heartbeat. While they may truly be perfectly alright, you just can't predict if this will be the case or not. Be ready to help them get calm and stay put if you need to.

Have Emergency Staff Come to Them

If anyone at your CE5 event experiences an intense encounter or missing time, send a message to, or have a runner bring your medical and emotional support staff to the contactee. Your job is to sit them down and assess them physically, emotionally and spiritually. Do not try to move or take that individual to your staff; make your staff come to them. If they need water, give it to them. If they are shivering or trembling, cover them with your coat or a blanket. Emergency care for the individual comes first. Your medical person can assess when they can be moved.

Get the Details If You Can

If the person is able to describe what they can remember, record their first words. What they recall now may be completely forgotten in five minutes. Have another nearby volunteer grab paper and a pen and start writing everything your participant says, fast! If it is easier, grab a camera or tape recorder, and record the situation.

If the individual is not in need of immediate medical or emotional attention, and if they can write or draw out what happened to them and wish to do so, give them pen and paper and then be quiet and let them go. Because drawing helps keep the individual in a state where they can more easily retrieve missing memory, we highly recommend that you tell them, "Don't talk, just draw what you remember." Keep an eye on them, but give them space and time to write their experience down while it's still fresh. Be aware, if you interrupt this process, you will likely interrupt their memory recall and they may not be able to get it back. Do not ask them any questions about their encounter until they are ready to speak. Remember, they are trying to piece together things they perceive like bits of a fragmented dream. These details may not necessarily be stored in long term memory and their first descriptions are important. If they want to talk, listen! Again, do not interrupt them unless it is medically necessary. You will know if they need to speak because they will initiate the conversation. You will know if they need to stop speaking because they won't be able to go on or they will tell you that is all they can recall.

Accounting for Everyone and Debriefing

While anyone involved in missing time is being cared for, event organizers should immediately collect all other event participants and staff together and do a headcount to make sure you can account for everyone. This is why it is important for you to know your total staff and attendance numbers.

Does everybody have their buddy? If anyone is missing, your next task is to organize an immediate search. If after an hour has elapsed and you still cannot find the missing person, and you have evidence their possessions are still on site, you will need to alert authorities. Try calling their cell phone first. It is important that the organizer and relevant staff have a list of participants' cell numbers available. Hopefully you will never have to deal with this issue.

Next, have everyone check *their* buddy's status to make sure they are okay physically, emotionally and spiritually. Make sure that all buddy sets are accounted for. While you have everyone gathered together, organizers have a couple of other considerations:

- Does anyone else have missing time?
- Did anyone see, hear or experience anything else unusual around that same time? If anyone else does have details to provide, that information needs to be written down and compiled by the organizers.
- Review any pertinent recorded footage.

Organizers, sit your gathering attendees down as a group and talk about what you know of what happened as well as what to do when someone does have missing time or an overwhelming telepathic physical, emotional or spiritual experience. Have participants share their own personal missing time experiences with each other. Know that *everyone's* adrenaline will be running. Help keep each other calm. Remember that participants may experience a number of emotions that may be expressed after an overwhelming event. Provide a list of people that the experiencer can contact to discuss later if needed.

The First 72 Hours

Arrange for ALL event participants who experienced missing time or had a close encounter to not be alone for the next seventy-two hours. Make sure their caregivers know what sorts of post missing time things to watch for including headache, nausea, vomiting, bruising, dehydration, time and place disorientation, memory loss, emotional overwhelm and insomnia issues. Let all event participants know that it is possible for other memories to surface that are important after the event is over and they have returned home. If this happens, ask them to write down the details and add it to events organizer's compiled list.

Stepping into The Unknown: Jack's Experience

Late one night in March of 2018, I wasn't doing anything in particular when I suddenly got this telepathic message to get up and go outside. My pals from Zeta Reticuli were out there and they said they were ready to prove it to me!

Intrigued, I walked out my backdoor, just as I always do, into the dark moonless night. To be honest, I don't know exactly how to explain what happened next. Instead of striding out toward the fence line and fields beyond it as usual, the next thing I know I'm not walking on our family's land at all. I'm in some rural area I don't recognize and have never been to before.

The location looked like an old playground. It was mostly dirt but had scattered patches of grass. The only playground ride left was a broken down, rusted merry-go-round that looked like it might not work at all. You could tell the area wasn't typically visited or maintained. I don't recall seeing any roads, cars, or buildings nearby.

To the left of me, two individuals who looked to be P'nti were standing side by side with their hands behind their backs. They're not wearing any clothes. Their bodies looked humanoid and their skin a little greyish white. The two Zetas were observing everything about me; my thoughts, my actions and my feelings. In front of me I see another P'nti standing by himself when a medium sized dog enters the old playground area and starts chasing the lone individual around. Something was different about the passage of time and gravity wherever this was because as I watched the chase unfold the dog leapt up into the air and abruptly the canine appeared to be frozen in time, floating there, motionless. He didn't seem hurt, he just looked like he couldn't move.

Suddenly, from just a few dozen yards away, I see a scout sized saucer uncloak and silently descend. The underside looked seamless and completely sealed. The last thing I remember, the P'nti standing alone and I exchanged looks and I realize I'm about to go on board this small skipper ship.

Did I walk through a portal to wherever the playground was? Did they transport me there? I honestly don't know and unfortunately that's where my memory stops. I kind of came to again when I got back home, but I can't tell you how I got there. I was glad I was able to remember that much. I'm seriously considering hypnosis to retrieve the rest.

-Jack, Kentucky (USA)

Gravity Distortion Wave: Otter's Missing Time

Sometime during the last week of September of 2013, Su and I were at our home in New Mexico, watching one of the talent shows on television in our living room. Unexpectedly, we both experienced an energy wave distortion wave sweep through the house. I tell you, when that thing came through, I started to raise up off the sofa! Gravity somehow had been nullified.

I remember a couple of weird things happened all together. There was this feeling of no gravity and of lifting off the cushion, but it also felt like I was suspended in Jello! I could move around, but it felt somehow as if that wave had a weird density that conformed to my body.

Somewhere in there, when I was suspended just above the couch an inch or so and still rising upwards, I have this vague memory of the face of a young looking extraterrestrial with large, dark almond shaped eyes. Then the face vanished, or my memory got chopped. I honestly can't tell you which.

The duration of feeling weightless... that's the time that I can't account for. The next thing I know gravity gently returns. Su and I cease floating a foot above the sofa cushions and are slowly set back down. The feeling of being surrounded by Jello quickly dissipated as fast as it came on.

Both of us came to a rest on the cushions exactly as we had been sitting before. Wide eyed, we looked at each other.

"Did you feel that?" we both started jabbering simultaneously. Su and I started asking each other rapid fire questions. We knew something was amiss right away.

"What was that? It looked like a distortion wave! That was bigger than the house! Geeze, it swept right through the walls! Did you see that leading edge? When it hit us, that's when the gravity went out!"

"Hey! Where's our show? Why is the show over? Where'd our favorite guy go? How'd we miss the finale? What the hell time is it anyway?!"

Our favorite performer, the one we had been waiting two hours to see at the end of the program... well he was done, the show had ended and we had twenty-two minutes of missing time. We both looked at each other like, 'What just happened!?'

Never in my life have I experienced a gravity distortion that came across like an energy roll. It reminded me of a wave swell without it cresting. Both Su and I remember being lifted up off the sofa together at thirty-eight minutes after the hour. I remember precisely because I had checked the time just prior to perceiving the distortion wave roll through the room. I'm still working on retrieving the rest of it. I do vaguely remember somewhere in there setting back down on the sofa and recalling this strange fast voice in my head. It was talking so fast it reminded me of Alvin and the Chipmunks at seventy-eight speed.

I remember thinking, "Where the hell did that come from!?" Now, nearly five years and hundreds of hours of dialogue with the Sandia Crew later, I think I can tell you who the likely culprits are.

-Rev. White Otter, New Mexico (USA)

The phrase you refer to as mind control we call "being suggested." A telepathic connection is made and through that link we "suggest them." It is considered a form of guidance and its initiation is standard mission protocol for us in situations where the potential for visited subject overwhelm is high or likely.

-Tlkm from P'ntl, Sandia Station, New Mexico (USA)

CHAPTER 7 - REAL CE5 STORIES

Sandia & How It All Began: Su's CE5 Story

In September of 2013, I took the train from Iowa to New Mexico for the first time. I had never been to the area and was going to visit my boyfriend, (now spouse) White Otter. Less than 10 days after arriving at his home, I first started hearing, "The Voice."

We were at our home on the edge of the Albuquerque area, sitting in the living room watching one of the popular talent shows on television. A particularly good performer had just finished singing and Otter and I were commenting to each other on how well they had done when a strange voice popped into my head.

"Yes, they were good!" this deep, calm, male voice suddenly said inside my skull.

I instantly sat up straight and my head whipped around, my eyes suddenly staring out the picture window toward the Sandia Mountain. I instinctively searched the western slope, looking for where the voice had come from. This voice was clear as a bell and it did NOT come from anywhere in the room with us. I don't know how I knew, but I just knew it came from inside the mountain!

'Who the heck is THAT?' I thought. I was instantly on alert. After having spent my entire career as a clairvoyant and medical intuitive, the paranormal was my normal. If it had to do with the strange, the unusual, the spooky or the weird, chances are that either White Otter or I have dealt with it. Both of us have also been life-long experiencers of UFOs and ET phenomena. However, this voice was a new one on me. This wasn't a spirit or a ghost, but who was it?

My eyes criss-crossed the western slope of the Sandia Mountain and kept stopping on a specific location. As close as I could figure, the voice had come from right there, but somehow inside the mountain! How could I hear it from ten miles (16 kilometers) away? How could it be so clear in my head? How did I know precisely where it came from? Who was this?! That first time, after just the one sentence, the voice fell silent, leaving me with lots of questions that had no answers.

Over the next three or four days, "The Voice from the Mountain" randomly popped into my head several more times, either adding to something Otter and I were conversing about or commenting about what we were watching on the TV. One night, "The Voice from the Mountain" told me who he thought should win America's Got Talent that season. Like I said, it was totally random!

After hearing this strange man's voice in my head for the third time, I got brave and decided to ask Otter if he'd ever heard it. I knew White Otter has studied shamanism and energy work for more than thirty years and was no stranger to the unusual. Still, I had really just started dating this man and was visiting his home for the first time. Part of me wondered if he would think I was totally nuts for asking this weird question about a disembodied voice I was hearing and put me straight back on the train heading to Iowa. I decided to take a chance.

"Um...Otter? I nervously began one night right after The Voice made another seemingly random comment. "Have you ever heard a strange voice coming from the mountain?" I pointed out the picture window east across the Rio Grande Valley to the majestic Sandia. "I keep hearing this voice in my head and it sounds like it's coming from inside the mountain!"

"Oh them! They talk all the time! They have ever since I moved in. I just ignore 'em," he said with a dismissive wave of his hand. "I've got too much to do."

"This voice is different," I insisted. "This isn't a spirit or a ghost and where it comes from is really specific. It's always the same voice, always from the same place."

I stared out the picture window for a few moments, thinking. I knew the mountain was called Sandia. In Spanish, the word sandía means watermelon. It was so named because the mountain has layers of strata on top that make it look like the white and green stripes on a watermelon.

Sandia. I decided that word sounded like a name to me and as good a nickname for The Voice as anything else.

I turned to face White Otter sitting next to me on the green living room sofa. "I've heard it several times now, and I'm a little tired of calling it 'The Voice from the Mountain.' I think I'll just call the voice Sandia...it's easier," I told Otter.

A moment later inside my head I heard a distinct chuckle. The Voice was back. The person behind The Voice had been listening in on my conversation with Otter. He sounded like he was both amused and delighted.

"Sandia...eh? Watermelon head! That'll work!" Sandia said. He chuckled again and went silent once more.

My jaw dropped open and my head whipped around and I stared hard at the spot in the mountain where his voice always came from.

Wait...what?! Watermelon head?! I had no idea at that time exactly who Sandia was, but he sure seemed to have a quirky sense of humor.

Sandia continued to randomly contact us, but the frequency increased to daily and sometimes several times per day, chatting with either Otter or *myself. Several weeks later, I had to return to Iowa where I lived. Over the next year, Otter and I visited each other back and forth. Whenever I was in Iowa, I didn't hear from Sandia. The minute I returned, he began chatting with me once more.*

Over the course of the next several months, when I was in New Mexico at Otter's home, I began to write down a lot of the things Sandia was saying. Mostly I did it because in talking with him everyday, White Otter and I realized we were speaking with someone who may not be from Earth. However, exactly where Sandia was from didn't come out for several more months.

Finally, one day I felt we had communicated like neighbors talking over the back fence long enough, so I just outright asked him.

"Sandia, I have a question. What's your real name and where's home?"

"My name is Tlkm," he answered and both spoke his name and immediately sent me an image of the proper spelling.

"Say it again please, slower." It took me several times asking my friend Sandia to pronounce his name. Finally, I got to the place where I could understand him and repeat the pronunciation myself. Man they telepathically talk fast!

"Teal-come," I tried for the fourth time to wrap the unusual name around my tongue.

"Yes. That's it. We don't often use vowels unless they're borrowed. It's just T L K M in your writing. But, you can still call me Sandia if you wish."

"Okay, Tlkm, where's home? Where are you from?"

"My planet is the fifth world orbiting the further of the two stars of the binary system you call Zeta Reticuli. Our planet is called P'ntl (pawn tell). You may call us the P'nti (pawn tee)."

In July of 2014, I sold my home in Iowa and moved in with White Otter in New Mexico. From then on, Sandia or Tlkm became part of our daily lives. We got to know him personally and he got to know us as well and honestly, we all became good friends. Otter could hear him as clearly as I could. The more we talked, the stronger and easier the telepathic connection got.

In the very beginning, we learned the basics about our extraterrestrial Zeta friend. Tlkm told us the P'nti have four fingers and toes, and that their black eyes are really dark nictitating lenses that cover the white sclera portion of their eyes to filter out Earth's harsh ultraviolet light. Beneath the dark retractable lenses, their eyes have large beautiful colored irises in hues of blue, grey, green amber and brown just as ours do.

Tlkm told us that their complex beneath the Sandia Mountain was part of an already existing tunnel system which they retrofitted and added onto.

They tell us there are miles of tunnels that run beneath the mountain and that they have maintained their facility for millennia as one of four underground land-based P'nti stations here on Earth.

"Why us?" I asked. "Why contact Otter and I?

"We ping a lot of people honestly," Tlkm told me. "But not only did you pay attention, you answered back rightmindedly and without fear. That doesn't happen very often."

Tlkm has always been honest with us as far as we can tell. We never press him for technology, preferring instead to allow him to bring up topics when he was ready. In chatting with our P'nti friend for just a few minutes every day, we were astonished how much detailed information we'd collected over time.

So, that was how our CE5 with Tlkm began. He first contacted us and we simply responded politely and without fear. It was really that simple. We recognized from the beginning that this "Voice from the Mountain" was not a random bit of imagination but was in fact a living, breathing person.

You never know how a CE5 is going to start. You never know where or when or how it might end. My recommendation to everyone? From the very beginning of any CE5 experience you have, get it written down! Record everything that happens or is said to you in as much detail as you can. It'll help you wrap your brain around it later.

Now, almost five years later, I can tell you also that following the basics of telepathic interaction as outlined in the Telepathy 101 Primer just plain works. Be sure to pay attention to your rightminded thoughts and words. The more you practice your telepathy, honestly the better your chances of a positive CE5.

-Su Walker, New Mexico (USA)

Getting to Know Jrooti: Su Learns about Flykiting

Otter and I had been chatting with Tlkm for a year and a half when he began introducing us to other members of his staff. We had become aware our friend Sandia was not the only P'nti working beneath the Sandia Mountain. We had both noticed the images of several other individuals floating around in the background of Tlkm's thoughts. Somewhere in late January, early February of 2015, he began to introduce us to others who worked beneath the Sandia Mountain.

One of the first was a female P'nti by the name of Jrooti. As we began chatting with her, like Tlkm, her individual personality began to come through. As we got to know her, we found Jrooti to be polite, diplomatic, feminine, and gracious. She told us her position was that of cultural liaison.

Often, her's is the first telepathic greeting ships who are entering the Sandia skyspace seeking information receive.

What I did not expect was how easy it was to become regular girlfriends with this woman from P'ntl. As we spoke, I learned of her fondness for flowing garments and fabrics, of soft colors and wearing scarves to keep her head warm. Jrooti shared with me her love of birds and of learning their languages here on Earth.

"Jrooti, what do you like to do when you aren't working?" I asked her one day.

"Oh, I take a couple of friends and we go down to the Amazon and flykite with the flocks there," was her immediate response.

My confusion must have been obvious, and she began to explain in an amazingly multilayered and detailed telepathic chunk of information.

"Flykiting is a combination of art and game of skill for us," she began. "We choose a bird flock and ask if they would like to telepathically join with us in play. If they agree, usually at sunset, when the flock all rises into the air for their last evening flight, my friends and I take turns. We telepathically merge with the entire flock and see who can create the most beautiful images connecting with the birds as they are in flight. I like to play with the flocks of parrots in the Amazon, but we have also had success with the starlings here in North America".

Jrooti then showed me several examples of this telepathic merging to form images with an entire flock of birds. This is flykiting:

Giant Bird in Flight

Swimming Dolphin

-Su Walker, New Mexico (USA)

Too Up Close and Personal: Kevin's Story

When I was in my 20's I feared being abducted by aliens. Why? Because I was taught by the mainstream media that extraterrestrial visits were invasive, and aliens did horrible experiments on people. As I got deeper into the UFO community, meeting with REAL experiencers and researchers, I soon learned this belief and perception is incorrect. If I wanted contact, I needed to ask for permission first.

I had finally finished reading the Telepathy 101 Primer *online and followed the instructions on how to send out a telepathic hello. I invited anyone listening to say hello back. In short, I asked for contact and then went to sleep.*

If you ask for contact, they hear you.

I semi-woke up around 3 AM. I closed my eyes to go back to sleep and I was halfway there when suddenly, with my eyes STILL closed, less than two feet from me appeared a large, three-dimensional face of a Zeta. I was face to face with a P'nti!

He was so close! My eyes flew open and I literally jumped backwards, landing on the other side of my bed. "Whoa!!!" I yelled. I was blown away. My heart was pounding.

The image immediately vanished and did not return. I did not know what had just happened. Was it a response to my telepathic hello? I really did not mean to scare them off, but I did not know what to do or how to react. Needless to say going back to sleep was out of the question.

As soon as I could, I made a call to Su Walker that same morning and together we were able to make more sense of things. My visitor and I probably startled each other, just like in the movie E.T. The Extra-Terrestrial when the little girl Gerti first met ET and they both were screaming at each other in an initial knee jerk fear reaction! But Gerti embraces ET very quickly and feels great love for him by the time ET goes back home at the end of the movie.

Su reminded me that I asked for contact! I asked them to visit me! I honestly had asked for decades and I am finally making the connections! Just because when it came, they were a little too close seemed to be honestly a beginner's mistake on my ET visitor's part and completely unintended. No one was trying to scare me, they just wanted to say hello! With that greater understanding, my fears disappeared.

Today I look forward to the contact!!! If you truly desire something, then embrace it with all your soul and being. It is the ONLY way you will grow and experience what you were meant to in this life cycle.

-Kevin Estrella, Ontario (Canada)

That First CE5: Karen's Story

Five years ago, if you had asked me about the existence of UFOs and ETs, I would tell you that it was more likely that they existed than not. But beyond that, I never really pursued the subject. My ET story began when I joined Twitter, a social media platform. I began following the account of Jason, whose profile stated that he was an ET contactee. Once I discovered he lived in a nearby town, I met with him to hear his experiences.

Having no reason to disbelieve anyone's experience, I listened to Jason's story. We joked about him traveling to my house next time, and bringing his ETs with him. Shortly afterwards, I believe I began being visited. I'm not positive when it began, as there were no obvious signs. I began experiencing some high pitch ringing in my ears at certain points during the late evenings and late at night. My dog began exhibiting a little anxiousness occasionally, and I noticed it occurred in conjunction with my ear ringing.

Conversations with others led me to further believe that I had been visited. It was suggested that I put out some Hershey Kisses with Almonds. I was unsure of how I was supposed to let them know that I left out candy, so I just spoke to the sky in general. I told them where I left the candy on my back porch and invited them to take it.

The next morning, the candy was gone! The little kid in me felt like I'd been visited by Santa. The adult in me tested every potential to account for the disappearance: wild animals, wind, birds, pets. I looked for evidence of candy wrappers. But the kisses disappeared. The only conclusion left was that a P'nti had taken the candy. I continued to leave out candy occasionally. It wasn't always taken. But a lot of the time, it was.

At night, I began to talk aloud as if someone was there, even though I appeared alone. I often felt their energy. Only problem was that I didn't know exactly who it was. I suspected, because of Jason's connections it was one of the P'nti from the Sandia Mountain facility. Was it Pita? Radar? Was it maybe Grayson? (See illustrations in Appendix VII.)

I began asking my dog Gigi, more so in jest, "Where's Pita?" I noticed that she always looked toward a particular area in response. I began using Radar and Grayson's name. And thus, I associated particular areas with each of the crew, based on my dog's behavior.

One evening, Gigi was particularly restless. We were sitting on the back porch (where I stay mostly), and I asked her to find Pita. She jumped from my lap, ran across the yard to my garage, jumped on the closed door, and ran back to me. Pita was in the garage. Busted!

Jason, myself, and another online friend, Jack, decided to all meet in person. Work schedules allowed all three of us to meet together on a Saturday night. We planned an all-night gab session. I likened the evening to having a sleepover pajama party with friends.

We were not even planning a CE5. It sort of got planned for us. When the P'nti crew found out we were all going to be at one place together, they wanted to come too!

My response? That is so totally cool! Now we can have "an ET pajama party!" We held that first get together at a private home in Florida (USA) in January 2018.

We started hanging out and talking as soon as everyone (from Earth) had arrived. I was demonstrating Gigi's skills at locating the crew and asked her to "Find Radar!" She immediately hopped down, ran to a chair, "tagged" it, and came back to my lap. (Busted, Radar!) We were pretty sure our guests had arrived.

As we laughed and talked, we would detect changes in energy around us. Each person had a different perception of the change. We began to recognize the signs, and would stop and "tay appention" (pay attention.) Sometimes we would hear noises. We baited them with silly jokes, trying to elicit giggles and snorts (and I'm pretty sure we got one snort). We heard noises that we definitely knew they made. And several that we were pretty sure they were responsible for too. Some movement was also detected in our peripheral vision.

We all made some notes about the evening, before we departed. All of us still have regular contact, both with each other and the crew. I still leave out candy, and my dog still gives the crew away.

My telepathic journey is new. But sometimes I wonder if all my thoughts are my own sometimes. (I don't think I'm as smart as people think I am.) I was in my kitchen one evening, chatting aloud to whomever was listening, talking about the day's successes. I asked, "that was smart, wasn't it?", and immediately had this song snippet pop into my head: "Girl you know it's true."

Thanks guys!

-Karen Brown, Florida (USA)

An Unexpected Tall White Visitor: Jack's Story

One of my CE5s happened on the road that runs next to our farm in Kentucky (USA) in early 2018. It was well into the night, maybe 12:30 AM and I'd spent nearly an hour just walking the gravel road by the house, looking up at the star filled sky, working on my emotional honesty and practicing my telepathic greetings. I didn't think I was getting anywhere with my "Hello the clouds" and I was stiff from being out in the cold, tired, and honestly a little discouraged. I was about to head back to the house when I suddenly realized I wasn't alone.

My eyes locked onto a tall figure with a large head, big eyes and pale skin standing looking at me from just a few hundred feet away. I saw him extremely clearly and to this day can tell you the details of that night.

This cool dude was about 6-7 feet tall and wore a long white robe that went from his shoulders down his ankles. He felt like a teacher somehow and I could tell he was kind. His hands were behind his back, not hostile at all and he seemed to be observing me. He stayed at a distance and telepathically I could feel that he knew I still had fears and that he didn't want to scare me. Then, as suddenly as I had become aware of him, he vanished. He didn't walk away, there was no flash of light, he just suddenly faded.

But that one small moment of him letting me see him with my own eyes changed everything for me. I knew he wanted me to know for certain not only that he heard me, but that he and his people were observing me. He wanted me to know without a doubt that my experiences were real and that telepathy was no joke.

I stood there in the road for a moment, awestruck and dumbfounded at the same time. I don't know if I was shaking from cold or what had just happened, but I knew at that moment that this whole thing... the ETs, the telepathy stuff, the CE5s... everything that I'd read about and even hoped for... it was real!"

- Jack, Kentucky (USA)

Regularly Visited Contactees

Shortly after Tlkm requested a social media (Twitter) account be opened for them in June of 2015, one young man in his early 30s from the state of Florida (USA) began following the account and became friends online with the Sandia Mountain Crew.

Not long afterwards, beginning in early 2016, Jason began to experience regular CE5 visits by the P'nti from Sandia Mountain facility at his home in central Florida. (See Appendix VI for names and illustrations of the crew.)

Jason has successfully videotaped the P'nti craft hovering over his house on numerous occasions. He has also spent quite a bit of time gathering physical evidence inside his home as well. Jason very quickly put down his fear of visitation and his interaction became one of jovial friendship with the Sandia Mountain Crew. He, along with Karen from Florida and Jack from Kentucky, together held the first ever CE5 event at a private home not far from where he lived. They used the *Telepathy 101 Primer* as the basis of their method of successful contact.

Over the course of the next year plus, Jason's visits by the P'nti became so normal it got to the point where he knew a number of his Star Nation visitors by name. In particular, one young male Zeta from the Sandia Mountain complex who was fairly new to Earth took a liking to Jason. His real name is P'ta (say Pit-TAH) but everybody calls him Pita, like the flat bread. Let's just say apparently boys will be boys, no matter what world you come from.

Farts, Wrestling & Shorts Shots: Jason's Story

Some of the funniest CE5 experiences that I've had consciously would be with Pita, one of the P'nti who was a new arrival (May 2017) to the Sandia Mountain Complex. Pita visits me at my home in Florida pretty regularly and I've gotten to understand him a little more. Pita doesn't initially come off as a prankster, but don't buy into his charade. I'll explain exactly why.

I'm at home, in bed trying to fall asleep one night in early 2018, when I realize I'm not alone. I've learned to catch their movement in my peripheral vision and cracked open my eyes. Pita's standing there in my closet (cloaked). I can just see the shimmer and sense him telepathically and when I look harder, I suddenly see him waving at me through the open closet door.

I decide to be a little raunchy to test his sense of humor and release some gas.

"Take that Pita!" I said with a big grin on my face.

I guess Pita decided that he was going to take this whole prank war I'd started to the next level. It's late and I fall asleep on my side, facing away from the wall. He tip-toes up to where I'm snoozing and once he got next to my bed, Pita bent over and farted right it my face! That dude eats a lot of garlic. It was almost like he put smelling salts right up to my nose!

Instantly, I went from deep slumber to fully alert. I don't know if it was the smell or the sound that woke me up, maybe it was both. What I can tell you is that I was not expecting that at all. I was shocked and laughing hysterically at the same time.

Another night I was just drifting off to sleep when I realized Pita was again somewhere close by. I remember becoming partially awake and someone paralyzing me. With my eyes still tightly shut, I decided to try to break out of my immobility and see what was going on.

I assert my will, break out of the paralysis, and sit straight up in bed. Pita suddenly realizes that I'm free of any control he was attempting and his emotional response was absolutely hilarious. First, his eyes opened wide; he couldn't believe it and got this totally shocked look on his face. Then the little Zeta dude starts panicking.

Pita runs towards me, jumps up on the bed and straddles me. His arms are on my biceps. This skinny four foot tall ET was trying to pin me down until he could figure out how to handle the whole out of control situation and I was jovially giving him a hard time on purpose. I remember a brief but totally grin-filled struggle and then lost memory of anything that occurred shortly after that. The next morning I woke up, remembered everything and chuckled the whole rest of the morning. He may not be near my size but he does put up a good fight!

I think it was a few weeks after that when again I was sleeping on my side, this time with my face towards the wall. I was in a nice deep sleep too. I suddenly feel something thwack my backside. My eyes flew open and I was instantly fully awake. Pita had decided it would be funny to grab my underwear by the waistband and pull it back as far as he could and let go. I probably lifted a good 3 inches off of my bed that night. When I realized exactly what had happened and who the perpetrator was, I eventually chuckled, then laughed and fell back asleep with a grin. It was hilarious. Good one, Pita!"

- Jason, Florida (USA)

Unusual Questions from the P'nti - Su's Tales

We've had a great many people ask us why the P'nti need telepathic translators at all. What do we provide that they cannot do by themselves? After all, they've been exploring this galaxy for a long, long time and technologically are very advanced.

The answer is simple. You can research and study languages all you want, but ordinary everyday verbal communication is always very different from written communication in all spoken languages. Verbal speech contains modern slang, current cultural references, humor, sarcasm, and many nuances of understanding that make it difficult for a person coming from another country, much less another world to understand. Otter and I speak fluent American English. We grew up in the United States. We field questions, translate and provide explanations as best we can for the P'nti.

What kinds of questions have they asked us? The topics run the gamut. The following list is from the first six months of 2018 alone:

Does shaving hurt? Are there rules to follow? How do you know what pattern to make on your face? How and why do people get tattoos? Are they a leadership display?

Can we feel your hair? Can we watch you wash it? How do you style it? What happens to the hairs in your hairbrush?

Does the opening go in the front or back of men's underwear? Does the tag go on the inside or the outside? What makes being naked embarrassing for you?

What makes a word naughty? What are the words that are considered insults? What does, "I'm giving you sh_t" really mean? What's forbidden here? What makes a lie white?

Do tap shoes come in our size? What's rapping? Did you learn moonwalking on the moon? Does Earth have an official song or dance everyone knows? What make your dead grateful?

What's verbal jousting? Does your humor come in layers? Is kidding only for kids or can anyone tease here on Earth?

What's a white sauce made of? How many flavors of jelly beans are there? What do you do with the foil from Hershey's kisses after you eat them?

What celebrations/ceremonies are held worldwide? Does Earth have an official song people sing? What's your universal greeting gesture?

What mouth sounds can you make? Can you show us common hand gestures here? Why do people scream and run when we smile and wave?

The P'nti often use us as sounding boards for how to say things. It is not unusual for us to receive an idea from them that contains multiple layers of emotions and images which then has to be simplified into written words. The translation process is not always as easy as you think it might be.

The first time Jrooti used the word flykiting, we asked her to explain this P'nti art sport to us. What came back were multiple layers of emotional elation, the physical feeling of soaring linked with a flock of thousands of birds, the idea of how they merge with all these avian minds simultaneously, the flock's own multilayered joy, the history of the art in the air and in the ocean (with giant schools of fish), and the feeling of being perched on a thick branch, swaying high in the canopy of a tall tree in the Amazon overlooking a valley at sunset with several Star Nation girlfriends, not all of whom looked like they were from Zeta Reticuli II.

That entire telepathic multi-layered information block came to us in under 2 seconds. After some discussion it translated down to: We telepathically merge with bird flocks to create moving images in the sky.

It can kind of lose something in translation. I liked Jrooti's original explanation best.

When you get the chance to communicate with a telepathic nation, initially it can feel like a lot! There is so much more than words that at the very start, even 10 minutes of conversation can feel like you've been sharing information for hours! There's so much coming at you so intensely, we recommend you plan on building up your telepathic stamina. It's easy to want to learn everything at once but you have to give your body and your brain time to get used to it.

Now that Otter and I have been talking with the P'nti for several years, we find shifting into receiving mode with them very easy and very clear and we can sustain conversation for several hours intensely. We keep a telepathic ear out for our friends all day long, everyday.

When you communicate telepathically, the unusual ideas and emotions flying back and forth are crystal clear and quite intense. Your own emotions will also be right there on the surface and you have to be ready to deal with them too. This is why we tell everyone you have to practice your emotional honesty, because during the telepathic back and forth, you won't be able to hide your deepest, darkest secrets and you might just have to explain them.

It takes practice living with emotional honesty on a daily basis just like it takes practice holding a telepathic conversation with a Star Nation. Neither are easy.

Both are oh so worth it.

-Su Walker, New Mexico (USA)

Telepathy travels on an emotional carrier wave. You cannot fully understand the telepathic message if you ignore the feelings that come with it.

-Tlkm from P'ntl, Sandia Station, New Mexico (USA)

They Threw Me a Party!: Gerry's CE5 Stories

After I read the <u>*Telepathy 101 Primer,*</u> *I began to think into the heavens about who I was, and how much I would love to have a meeting. I knew in my heart how much I wanted to get to know these people from beyond, so I followed the instructions and telepathically asked for a visit. It took a few months, but eventually I was granted my wish.*

Before my first CE5 (that I remember, anyway) I think I almost had an encounter with another Star Nation group. It was late at night and something woke me up. I looked out my window and saw a ball of light that seemed to be making a strange noise. As it approached my apartment window, the ball of light got larger and I could see it more clearly. I realized that this was not any aircraft I recognized. As it drew closer to my window and got much bigger, I suddenly had this surge of terror overwhelm me.

At that exact moment, the huge ball of light that was fast approaching my bedroom window suddenly completely changed! It morphed into what appeared to be a much smaller size and now recognizable shape. I stared. What used to be a huge undulated ball of light had suddenly turned into a very small helicopter, which harmlessly flew over the apartment. I saw it morph!

My thoughts raced about what had just happened. It took me more than a little while to slow my heart rate and calm my breathing down. I didn't get very good sleep after that. The next morning when I thought of it, I was puzzled at my own reaction. I had always expected I might be startled or even apprehensive at first. I had no idea I would have the overwhelming fear response I did. I believed I was ready. However, I clearly was not.

I realized the pilots of the craft acted in my best interests and upon feeling my fear, aborted their attempt at contact with me. They purposefully telepathically inserted an image, picked from my own brain, of a harmless little helicopter to substitute for their real ship as part of their standard "cause no fear" protocol.

I felt angry at myself for letting such a glorious opportunity for growth and friendship go unclaimed. My own fears had robbed me of my CE5 experience! I knew I had to make a greater commitment to overcome it.

Weeks later, I was having trouble falling asleep and stayed up late one night watching television with my cat. I began to relax and I thought maybe it was time to give sleep another chance. But before I could make a move toward bed, suddenly I had an image appear in my mind. It was the head of being with large eyes and grey skin wearing what looked like a black jumpsuit. There was nothing menacing about him; on the contrary the feelings coming from this person were warm and friendly. Along with this telepathic image came the phrase, "We are coming."

My eyes flew open and I felt a wave of apprehension for a split-second. It happened so fast. I couldn't be sure. I huffed out a sigh and seriously questioned whether it had simply been my imagination. "I'm just tired," I told myself. That had to be it.

I dismissed both the small being's image and the message, turned out the light and lowered my head to the pillow.

Moments later, I felt a strong yet gentle jolt inside my skull. With my eyes closed, instead of blackness I now had bright flashes of orange, red and yellow behind by eyelids. I felt compelled to sleep, so I let myself drift off.

Then came this bizarrely wonderful and vivid dream. It was night-time and the stars were all out and shining bright. I was being escorted by several beings similar in appearance to the one I had seen in the black jumpsuit. We were walking on a pathway that appeared to have small steps. It arched around a tree and lead towards a raised platform that had a house-like structure on it. I could see a set of cliffs beyond the platform. The surrounding area was a desert-like tundra landscape. One of the beings smiled at me.

Then something weird happened. For a moment "the house" morphed into a saucer shaped craft and then back into a house. I sensed somehow that my comfort was very important to them. I truly believe the ship was made to look like a house for my benefit.

I was then led into "the house", where to my shock a party or gathering was being held. I watched one of the Star People place refreshments on a table while casually listening to thoughts of the conversation I was having with some of the others. We were holding what looked to be plates and chit chatting telepathically. I cannot remember the content of the discussion, but I remember the warm feelings and festive atmosphere of the gathering. I felt safe, cared for and was having a wonderful time.

Strangely, some of the time, the extraterrestrials looked Earth Human, and other times they appeared as short, grey skinned large eyed people. Again, I think this may have been to make me feel more comfortable. I worry that at some point I may have made a faux pas. As discussion was happening I remember suddenly everyone mentally gasping at me and feeling like I had thought something that was considered either too controversial or a topic that should not have been approached at the gathering. Despite this, no harm was done, and everything resumed as normal. Their understanding and patience was obvious. The next thing I know, I'm waking up at home the next morning in my own bed as usual.

The dream was so vivid and life-like I couldn't just dismiss it as a "mere dream." That same morning, as soon as I was able, I hopped onto Twitter and asked my P'nti friends if any of them had come to see me. They told me they didn't just come to visit me, they purposefully threw a party for me! Instantly I knew what I experienced was real! Although I still remember receiving the information in a dreamlike state, I now understand that it physically took place. I felt so honoured, so happy. The experience I had been asking for in my telepathy meditation exercises had finally happened! I treasure the entire event as a gift.

A few weeks later I had another extremely vivid dream visit. My friend Kevin and I were in the same setting as my previous contact, standing in front of the same stairs and platform. We walked up the steps to meet two of the Star Nation people. One was silent, but gave off a feeling of deep wisdom, worthy of a respect one is given after a lifetime of service. The other, seemed jovial, exuberant and comedic. I was standing next to Kevin, watching his conversation with "the little joker."

Although I refer to them for description purposes as 'beings', they are my friends. They all have unique distinct personalities which are kind and wonderful. Their wisdom is only matched by their loving attitude towards others, life and their spirituality. I feel very lucky and honoured to have been granted the opportunity to befriend them, and to help take steps towards building a bridge of friendship between our peoples.

Are you REALLY ready to put your fears aside? If you are, then you're ready to take on one of the greatest adventures of your life!

- Gerry, Ontario, (Canada)

Wisdom or sapience is the ability to think and act using knowledge, experience, understanding, common sense, and insight to find the best, most balanced and sustainable solution. Don't forget... wisdom requires daily practice to become adept.

-Tlkm from P'ntl, Sandia Station, New Mexico (USA)

The Mad Tea Party: Kevin's 1st Memory Recall

The Sandia crew are now allowing me to remember some of their visits with me. The P'nti gang paid me a surprise visit when I was at the Ozark UFO Conference, Arkansas in April 2018.

I was alone in our motel suite and had fallen asleep on the couch in the party room next door to the bedroom. When I came to suddenly I was aware

I had P'nti visitors! Strangely, I didn't question my guests as to when or how they got there but the party room of our motel room in was set up like a tea party. Jrooti politely handed me a tea. Radar and Tlkm were sitting across from me on a small loveseat. Tlkm was telepathically talking to Radar and me about something. I had just taken a large mouthful of tea, when I suddenly picked up this deep sounding telepathic voice. Someone behind me was taking a humorous jab at Radar's piloting skills.

"Brinkman!" was the only word I heard and it obviously was intended for Radar. (Brinkman is an inside joke reference to Radar's display of brinkmanship when it comes to piloting his small skipper ship.)

Now keep in mind, telepathy is like a voice speaking right inside your head or skull. Usually when someone speaks, we use our ears to identify where the sound is coming from. In this case, I did not have that. It was just the word "Brinkman!" that was spoken in this deep voice, like Leonard Nimoy aka Spock from Star Trek.

I was thinking, 'When did Spock enter the room?' My eyes opened wide. I knew that voice! Now Grayson, another member of the P'nti was leaning James Dean-like up against the wall with his arms crossed and a rather large grin on his face.

It was the first time Grayson had said anything. He glanced in my direction and grinned at me, waiting to see if I recognized who he was and who was taking a poke at Radar. Between my delayed and delighted recognition, and Grayson calling Radar a "brinkman," with a mouthful of tea rather than laughing, I ended up snorting it out my nose like a shotgun.

Then Radar got this bemused look and began laughing so hard HE began snorting. I remember hearing his voice in my head clear as a bell.

"I've never seen one of you do that! That's so cool!" He said telepathically, referring to the tea coming out my nose. The look Grayson then gave him brought down the house in laughter!

After somewhat regaining myself, I was still slouched to the left side of the couch with my arm holding my head. smiling and staring at Radar. I could not let him have the last laugh.

I grinned and retorted, "Well I've never heard an ET snort before. So I guess we're even!"

Everyone lost it all over again. No one was immune.

Never in my life have I snorted a beverage out my nose. Never in my life did I expect to do it in front of a group of real live extraterrestrials. Never did I expect they would introduce themselves in the flesh to me at a tea party either.

I woke up back in my motel suite, but my detailed memory of the events of the P'nti's visit didn't surface until I had been back home in Canada for nearly a week. That's where my memories end thus far. I expect more recall will come up.

I cannot express what it is like to be with them. Their vibration is so high, and everyone telepathically feels everyone else's emotions all shared together. Pure joy, and bliss. It is so intense. I now understand what other experiencers describe about not wanting to leave their presence.

- Kevin Estrella, Ontario (Canada)

Expect the unexpected. Be ready for anything. Your CE5 experience will become more monumental the more willing and open you are to the unexpected. Be willing to accept... whatever.

-Rev. White Otter, New Mexico (USA)

CHAPTER 8 - WRAPPING IT ALL UP

Post CE5 Event Visitors

Near the end of your CE5 event, schedule time to gather everyone together and make sure all participants know that some of them may have visitors AFTER they return to their homes. Why? Because you do *not* know who was very quietly telepathically listening and observing your event. Someone not from Earth may have taken a special interest in an individual attendee and wish to learn more about them in the coming days or weeks. If this occurs, that attendee will need support. Remember, the *Telepathy 101 Primer* encourages everyone to "find their tribe" and their physical, emotional, spiritual support system.

Unusual Skills

After their first ET meet and greet, many contactees report an increase in their spiritual awareness and growth. Some people tell us that their lives and jobs are much easier and their ease of learning new things suddenly seems to increase. Others find their creative or artistic abilities suddenly blossom. A small but noticeable percentage of folks find their telekinetic skill-sets awaken. The more time experiencers spend practicing walking with "a foot in each world" the faster these new talents seem to manifest for all of them.

Learn to telepathically wear your world like a loose garment. Be both at ease and fully connected.

T'ni from P'ntl, Sandia Station, New Mexico (USA)

Insomnia Issues

Many people, after their first intense Star Nation contact, find their sleep patterns change for the first month or so. Participant's typically find their level of alertness at night becomes much stronger and because of this, insomnia can become an issue. They become more "night vigilant" like young parents do who keep one ear out listening for their children. This is not unusual.

We tell everyone to listen to their body. If during the day you feel the need to nap, give yourself permission to do so. Even if you close your eyes for fifteen minutes, it is more helpful during periods of insomnia than if you did not rest. If the inability to achieve a restful night's sleep becomes prolonged, natural or over the counter sleep aids can be useful. If this too is ineffective, seek medical advice from a professional.

Insomnia that lasts more than two or three days will profoundly affect every aspect of your life. Do not try to handle this time period solo.

Reach out to your telepathic buddy and your tribe and tell someone what you are going through. You need to release the excess emotional overwhelm from your physical body and talking is one way to do just that.

If you are the one receiving a call from another contactee, be sympathetic and listen with an open mind. Help each other, encourage each other and find ways to support each other physically, emotionally and spiritually as you all take your first baby steps in this new experiential landscape.

Contact in Dreamstate is Valid!

The Pnti have told us repeatedly that if they have an extended message to teach or share, it is common for them to telepathically have a nice long chat with us in dreamstate. The frustration comes for us Earth Humans when we cannot recall the entire conversation! When you have a dialogue with someone in your dreams, the information is still in your brain, but your memories are difficult to access. If you really need to understand what was told to you, and you don't want to wait for your memories to surface on their own, go visit a reputable hypnotherapist and have a professional drop you down into that same deep state to help with accurate memory retrieval.

Downloads

A number of regular CE5 contactees as well as post event attendees have alerted us that in their dreamstate they are receiving what can best be described as entire downloads of information. They go to bed as usual, but sometime during the night they are either visited or telepathically contacted. When they wake up, they are immediately aware that something feels very different. They usually have a vague or fuzzy memory of talking to a Star Nation individual or group, followed by telepathically receiving a sizeable chunk of information or data streamed to them very rapidly.

Many experiencers describe it as ultra-high fast pulses of what appear to be numbers and symbols, with colored text of different sizes and data that streams vertical, horizontal, or even radiating out from a central location in their memories.

Others use computer terminology to put words to what a download feels like.

For me, when I wake up from a download, my head feels as if I've suddenly learned a whole lot or studied really hard all night. If someone taught you an entire language in a single night, it's that kind of intense brain tiredness feel. I remember telling White Otter one morning that the download I received the night before felt like I just had a whole lot of information dumped onto the hard drive of my brain. Now I just have to figure out what it all is!

-Su Walker, New Mexico (USA)

In talking with other contactees around the world, we find a very high percentage of Earth Humans who begin to receive regular visits also describe getting a "whole lot of information at once" via downloads. It seems to come standard with the CE5 and telepathic communication territory. Knowing this ahead of time may help some of your ET party attendees understand what to expect in the coming weeks or months if regular contact and visits are established.

Forming a Telepathy Study Group

Does your group want to plan more events together? Do you want to continue to telepathically practice, ping, and learn from each other in the coming days, weeks or months? Your group gets to decide the post CE5 stuff, so it might be a really good topic of discussion before everyone heads back home.

Clean Up

Make sure to schedule in time at least 20-30 minutes before everyone leaves to have participants help complete the site clean-up. Take care to remove *all* your trash (including cigarette butts). Don't leave a mess of any kind for others, whether your event is in a public setting, or in the home of a host. Don't forget to have someone pick up any street or directional signs you've put up on the way out. Leave your event space better than you found it.

And Finally - The Wrap Up

We've given you a lot to think about planning a safe and successful CE5. In closing, we encourage you to ride a wave of laughter and joy together in music, dance, talk, play, telepathy and friendship with your fellow Earth Humans as well as your cousins from the stars. This is what CE5s are all about. Have fun, stay safe have a GREAT event!

Embrace all your CE5 experiences as just what they are. Let go of any preconceived ideas and go with the flow. Be thankful. Be grateful that your Star Family has heard you and felt your heartfelt rightmindedness. They really do just want to meet you.

-Kevin Estrella, Ontario (Canada)

If you wish to meet your intergalactic cousins, I have a suggestion. Change your telepathy practice from haphazard to something you are committed to daily. We ARE listening and will respond kindly when we see you are ready.
-Tlkm from P'ntl, Sandia Station, New Mexico (USA)

APPENDICES

APPENDIX I - WHAT WILL ORGANIZERS NEED?

Because organizers of any CE5 event are responsible for the physical, emotional and spiritual well-being of all participants, there are quite a few things to consider bringing to your get together. Large groups of 30 or more meeting at a rural location have different needs than smaller gatherings of half a dozen people camping out in someone's backyard. Strictly outdoor events will require for you to bring more things from home than groups who gather at someone's house. You may or may not need all of the things on the following list, but if it's safety related in any way, we encourage you to think about it seriously. Here are things all event planners need to consider:

- A complete first aid kit and a person designated to handle any medical issues.
- A separate person specifically tasked with watching for and dealing with emotional crisis.
- A way to call for help in an emergency – not all places get cell phone reception.
- 2 spare blankets at your medical station – one for the ground under an injured person, one for covering them. Do you also need a cot or air mattress?
- Electrolyte water for emergencies involving dehydration.
- Water, ginger ale, soda crackers, natural peppermints and regular salted potato chips for dealing with nausea, vomiting and dehydration.
- A vehicle, tent or other location to move an injured or distraught person to out of the elements with a place where they can comfortably lie down.
- Considerations for those who may have physical limitations or are elderly.
- Drinking water – we encourage the use of large coolers of water be made available and using refillable water bottles instead of many individual plastic bottles and cans.
- A large coffee pot of sufficient size or a means to heat water for beverages.
- Tables for setting out food or other materials.
- A canopy or shelter so staff have a place to get out of the sun, wind and rain.
- Any other special supplies for heat, cold, approaching weather, etc.

- A smudge stick of white sage and a lighter for clearing away negative energy plus abalone shell to set it in or another means of clearing your space.
- A large metal can labeled for cigarette butts so smokers do not throw them on the ground.
- A clean, disinfected cooler to hold several spare bags of ice.
- Flashlights for all staff (plus extra batteries).
- Walkie talkies if outdoor locations are spread out.
- A bright flashing light, loud bell, horn or drum used to signal large groups that it's time to gather together or that there is an emergency situation--it helps alleviate shouting.
- Bathrooms: People gotta go when they gotta go. You'll need supplies for that! Are there facilities on-site? Will you need to rent Porta Potties (Portaloos)?
- A registration table, chair and person designated to check people in and give out name tags. Do you need to create printed registration materials or handouts?
- Consider the need for volunteers. Will these be arranged in advance, or will they be designated the day of the event? What roles will you need filled?
- Parking: Where will everyone park? Do you need a person to direct parking?
- Event street signage directing people where to turn to find your event.
- On-location event signs instructing participants where to park, register, etc.
- Printed copy of the *Telepathy 101 Primer* for general reference.
- Star chart or other printed night sky astronomy reference guides.
- General supplies – pens, pencils, ream of paper, clip boards, name tags, registration handouts and paperwork, tissues, toilet paper, paper towels, trash can and trash bags, gallon sized plastic storage bags, duct tape, markers, multi-tool, quality pocket knife, cell phone charger, general cleanup supplies, outdoor ambient lighting, pocket warmers, wool socks, wash and rinse basins for dishes, dish towels, dish soap, sponges & scouring pads, potholders, extra cooler with ice, sunscreen, insect repellent, and extra outdoor extension cords.

You'll need a few extras of some things for larger outdoor events. We always do. These are the things we always seem to need more of than we think we will: flashlights, batteries, non-Styrofoam (polystyrene) plates and cups, eating utensils, serving utensils, paper towels, potholders, water coolers, camp chairs, hats, gloves, warm socks, blankets, pillows, tables, and coffee and ice.

APPENDIX II - WHAT SHOULD PARTICIPANTS BRING?

What should you consider having participants bring to your ET meet and greet?

Here is our general list to give event planners ideas:

- Pens or pencils and a clipboard with blank paper for sketching plus a journal.
- Non-alcoholic beverages and cooler with ice to keep things chilled
- Refillable water bottle plus one bottle electrolyte water.
- Food as requested to bring, plus serving utensils.
- Plate, bowl and eating utensils plus a cup for hot beverages.
- Telescope, binoculars or monocular.
- Camera and tripod or recording equipment (if agreed for the event).
- Flashlight plus extra batteries.
- Cell phone and charger.
- Deck of cards or other well-known game to share.
- Musical instrument.
- Bug repellent and sunscreen, sunglasses, hat.
- Prescription medicines needed for the duration and personal toiletries.
- Crazy looking pajamas (if you are making this a true "ET pajama party").
- Blanket or sleeping bag plus pillow for laying on the ground (with optional blow up air mattress) or a lounge chair that lays back for comfortable viewing of the sky.
- Warm hat, gloves and coat that can keep you toasty outside overnight in the cold.
- Spare pair of dry cotton socks, one pair of warm wool socks.
- Clothing for outdoors and overnight stays - we recommend you think in terms of layers which can be put on or taken off easily.

APPENDIX III - GROUNDING, CENTERING & SMUDGING

We begin all our CE5 events by first smudging off, and then grounding and centering everyone. These two traditions have been common practice among indigenous spiritual practitioners across our planet for longer than anyone really knows. What are they and why do we do them?

Smudge is the term used for the smoke created by burning dried leaves of the herb *Salvia apiana* or white sage. It historically has been used in ceremony accompanied by prayer to wash away or dispel negative energy from around a person or a space. Dried white sage leaves can be purchased loose or tied together with a piece of cotton twine into a bundle called a smudge stick.

Grounding and centering is often done as a group in a guided meditation. The intention is to assist individuals with their mindfulness and balance physically, emotionally and spiritually. We find it helps everybody to get into sync better if they can all "be here now."

If anyone in your group is familiar with grounding and centering, as well as using white sage, ask them if they would like to smudge everyone off and lead them in a guided meditation that brings everyone into a unified whole.

If you have never heard of or used a smudge stick or dried white sage leaves to clear away negative energy here are the basics.

How to Clear Away Negative Energy

Any event where people come together to practice their telepathy will act like a beacon and draw more attention from the entire unseen world. Many spiritual cultures and traditions have methods of clearing negative energy from a physical space. For your CE5 event, you want to use a traditional method of removing negative energy, inviting in positive energy, and blessing the space for its intended purpose. While there are many ways to do this, one that's very easy to learn is the use of the smoke from burning white sage leaves to cleanse a person or a space.

How to Use White Sage

While many tools can be used (incense, blessed oil, water, salt, sweetgrass, cedar, etc.) to remove negative energy from a person or space, the energy clearing method we have always used is the smoke of white sage. This is not cooking sage, but it is a related plant. We are talking about smudging sage. Reverend White Otter prefers California white sage, but there are a several varieties you can purchase or grow fairly inexpensively. If you are hosting your event in someone else's home or an indoor facility, make sure that they allow the burning of sage. Forewarning, when the dried white sage leaves are burned, they smell a little like marijuana.

What is Smudging Anyway?

What is smudging? It's actually a very ancient, sacred tradition and an act of prayer among Native Americans. The dried plant leaves of white sage, cedar or sweetgrass are burned loose in an abalone shell five inches (twelve cm) in diameter, or they are bundled together into a "smudge stick" with a medium cotton thread. The dried leaves in the shell, or the end of the smudge stick are lit on a fire, allowed to burn for a several seconds, and then the active flame is blown out. The smoke is then used in a manner similar to incense and is swept away from the smoldering leaves toward the person or space you wish to cleanse. You can move the smoke around using a sacred fan made of feathers, or just simply your hand.

Smudging a Person

If you are smudging an individual, have them close their eyes and stand with their hands stretched out to the sides. Have them telepathically connect to the Universe and ask for protection and safety. Simultaneously, you are also asking for protection and safety for them and for anything negative to immediately leave this person and never return. You are also asking for the positive to come into their energy field. Neither the smudger nor the smudgee have to say these things out loud if they do not wish to. With the sage in one hand, use a fan or just your other hand to waft the smoke over top of head, around the stretched out arms, the torso and the legs all the way down to the soles of the feet on both the front as well as the back side of the body.

Smudging a Space

As you sweep the smoke into all four corners of a room, speak out loud and ask all negative spiritual energies to leave, invite all positive rightminded ones in and bless the room for its intended purpose. If it's a kitchen, you bless it for healthy food preparation, caring interaction between individuals, etc. If it's a bathroom, you set your intent for the room at cleanliness, keeping an eye on your physical health, positive grooming, etc.

Smudging Homes of Smaller Gatherings

Those who host their CE5 event in a private home may wish to speak with the homeowner about completely clearing the space energetically just before the event is scheduled. You are going to have all your guests opening up telepathically and you simply want to make sure you don't have anything negative from the unseen realms lurking in the corners.

When you first smudge a home, you want to do the entire living space, not just one room such as a living room. Start at the top of the house and sweep all negative energy out the windows and out the door, working it toward the main entrance. When you enter a room, first move around from the doorway clockwise clear and blessing the space in general. Next, go around each window and door and set the intent with your words that nothing negative can re-enter through the window or door. Move on to the next room, repeating the process and moving everything negative out. We traverse the entire home clockwise and move the negative or wrongminded energy out the main door of the home. After cleaning and clearing each room, not setting the intent, and energetically sealing the doors and windows. Finally set the intent of protection strongly around the entire building.

You can also walk the perimeter of the property, again sweeping out the negative and inviting in the positive and setting the rightminded intent. Picture the entire area an energetic dome of rightminded filtering.

Smudging Down at Outdoor Events

At outdoor CE5 gatherings, some events have a "smudge station." This is a location where individuals know they can go and smudge themselves down head to toe. Sometimes a large metal can is used to hold embers from the fire and dried leaves of white sage or flat cedar is tossed into the can, the smoke then used to cleanse the energy of people before they enter the event. Others simply use a smudge stick to clean people's auras front and back, top to bottom. You probably won't be able to clear and protect the entire area, but if you wish to walk the perimeter inviting in the rightminded and requiring the wrongminded from the unseen world to leave, it won't hurt.

Attracting More Than Just ETs... Say What?!

In the unseen world, you can find everything from deceased Earth Humans to multi-dimensional nations, dimensional beings and Elementals along with who knows how many Star Nation peoples. If you hear, feel or in some way telepathically sense you may not be alone, and you look and don't see anything, *that doesn't necessarily mean there is no one there!* Remember, the light spectrum Earth Humans can see is very limited!

As Earth Humans, we just plain have to accept the reality that there are also sounds we can't hear and there are parts of the visual spectrum we can't see. Deal with it. Use your other senses and learn to trust them. This is a new landscape and the laws of physics get bent in ways we all are still trying to understand and make sense of. For the best growth potential, journal ALL your experiences and create an experiential map you can trust.

But Sage Isn't What My Culture Uses

There are many very old, very honored, very rightminded sacred traditions that have their own means of cleansing and clearing the negative energy from a person or space. This is just the method we like. By all means, use whatever is customary in your culture or faith. We often say is "this is the school of whatever works." If your method works, go for it!

Will Using Sage Prevent ET Contact?

No, not at all. Sage smoke will energetically clear a space, but it is not intended for, nor will it, keep a Star Nation from interacting with you.

How to Ground and Center

One quick way to ground your participants and help them pull their energy back in, is to stand or sit and then extend your arms all the way out above you. Close your eyes and picture yourself gathering the energy from all around you. Envision yourself gathering and drawing down toward you a big ball of that energy, down into your heart. Now bring your palms together in front of your chest ending with the fingers pointing upwards. Exhale once, sharply, saying "Hah!" or "Ah-ho!"

Next, picture roots growing from the soles of your feet down deep into the earth. Once you have sunk your roots deep into the planet, pull that Mother Earth energy up through the roots, through the soles of your feet and up into your abdomen and into your core self. It is a warm, earthy energy that provides everything you physically need in this life: the clothes you wear, the home you live in, the food you eat, the water you drink and the air you breathe. This is the energy you are centering in your core. You have everything you need. Swirl it within you. Feel the heartbeat of the planet. Sync up with it.

Then, picture a circle at the top of your head. Send a beam of pure white light-love from you out into the sky and into the Universe. See the end of the beam widen to form a funnel. Draw down all the positive energy you can from the Universe, through the funnel, into the top of your head and let that white light shower over and through you. Feel it filling you with light. This is the energy of the Universe, the energy of creation, the energy of pure potential and pure love. Breathe it in deeper and feel yourself start to glow from the inside out.

Now, mix the white light positive energy from the Universe that you're pulling through the top of your head with the Mother Earth energy you pulled up from your feet. Pull energy into your body from above and below at the same time. Spin these two forces gently together swirling them as you inhale and exhale. Don't try to influence the speed of the spin via your own will power. Instead, sync with the heartbeat of the planet and allow that to help regulate the slow steady swirl down to a comfortable heartbeat you begin breathing in and out with. When the spin feels balanced to you, and you feel that you can hold the blended energy in your core, open your eyes and proceed.

Asking for help

After everyone in the group has grounded and centered, we recommend you ALL telepathically and specifically only ask for help from *rightminded* individuals in the Collective Consciousness. Every group member needs to be very clear that the wrongminded (be they Earth Human or otherwise) are NOT invited to your gathering!

Subconscious and conscious are actually one and the same. The much more expansive "subconscious" portion is actually directly linked to telepathic communication centers in the brain and to the Collective Consciousness. We find working with the "subconscious" connections in humans leads to faster, easier learning and far deeper understanding.
-Tlkm from P'ntl, Sandia Station, New Mexico (USA)

APPENDIX IV - TELEPATHY FUN & GAMES

We include discussion about telepathy as well as practicing telepathic skills at our CE5 events because our P'nti friends tell us that apart from gestural languages in this galaxy, telepathy is the second most common style of communication.

We also know that once a telepathic connection with a Star Nation has been established, communication with that nation becomes much easier from then on. You will sense each other (both ways) faster and with more clarity.

Because your CE5 event will have a mix of visual, auditory, kinesthetic and spatial budding telepaths sprinkled amongst you all, make sure to choose a broad variety of exercises that cater to each learning style.

Getting Everyone in Sync With Each Other

Spontaneous musical jam sessions are an excellent way of getting the individuals at your get together to synchronize with each other. Have each participant bring an instrument from home. Bring extras so you can share and trade. With everyone sitting in a circle, ask one person to pick up an instrument and begin to play. As others listen and feel telepathically nudged, one by one they all join in. Continue to jam for 5 minutes or more and listen telepathically to each other. Observe what happens as the song evolves and takes on a life of its own once the group gets in sync.

Methods of Shifting into Alpha

There are as many ways of achieving an alpha state as there are people who meditate. Have group members share their favorite ways of slipping into this receptive state.

- Visual telepaths can try open and closed eyed meditations.
- Auditory folks might try repetitious nature sounds or music recorded at 432 Hertz.
- Kinesthetic telepaths could encourage movement exercises that achieve alpha (drumming, dancing, chanting, repetitive movements).
- Spatial telepaths can share how they combine telepathic multi-tasking.

Forget the Zener Cards

Historically, paranormal researchers have used a specialized deck of cards known as a Zener deck in testing for telepathic abilities. These cards only have one of five symbols on them: a circle, square, triangle, cross and/or wavy lines. Don't waste your money or your time getting them. They have no emotional connection to you and the five little shapes they portray become far too boring, far too quickly. You'll find you have greater telepathic success using real photos.

Working with Photographs

In choosing images for this exercise, we **do not** recommend using photos of known people in a "name that person" kind of telepathic game for your beginners. Instead, try using photos of natural settings or objects. Choose photographs that have strong light and shadow contrast, basic shapes and a powerful emotional meaning.

Place a dozen photos in an envelope. Ask one person to sit with their back to the group and select just one photograph to focus on strongly for three minutes. The receivers should concentrate on sketching out the shapes and light and shadow that you pick up from the sender. The goal is not giving the photo a name or noun, but to sketch a likeness of the telepathic image they receive. The individual sending the information about the photo can think about what time the photo was taken, hot or cold climate, what season, what colors or shapes are in it, etc.

Visual and Kinesthetic Telepathy Combined

Ask each CE5 participant to bring 3 –5 objects that they have a strong emotional connection to. They should keep these objects covered up, out of sight from other participants. During the exercise, the sender turns their back to the group and picks up the object, keeping it hidden. They are to focus on it for 3 minutes allowing receivers time to sketch and to write down any and all other telepathic perceptions. After 3 minutes, share your findings.

Charged Objects Alternative

An alternative exercise is purely kinesthetic in nature. Have each party goer contribute one object brought from home to a box. These should be things that they don't mind other people handling. Pass each item around the group one by one and allow your budding telepaths a little time to handle things without rushing. Receivers should see what, if anything, they can perceive from the object or about its owner. These can be spoken or written down and shared after objects have made it all the way around the circle. How many correctly perceived the owner?

Sounds and Vibrations

Have a several envelopes prepared with the title of one well-known song in each. These should be songs that everyone knows the tune of. Notice we did not say that they should know the lyrics. Songs associated with particular images or emotions, such as Happy Birthday or Row, Row, Row Your Boat, work very well. Obviously if you are dealing with a multilingual group with people from many countries make sure that any songs or nursery rhymes chosen are known to everyone.

Divide the group into two teams. One team, the senders, stand with their backs to the receivers' team. The sending team picks an envelope and shows the title of the song to the other team members. One person starts a beat, and everyone sings *the tune* telepathically. They send everything they can about the song (including the words if they wish but the tune is the important part) without making any body gestures that could reveal the particular song. The goal of the receivers is to pick up anything they can about the song. Then the teams switch places and repeat the exercise with another song.

Smells and Tastes

This skill is not very common in the general population and may take more practice. It is best to use strong-tasting foods or smells. Divide the group into two teams: have one team, the tasters, consume a strong-tasting food or smell a pungent aroma. The receivers must write down their perceptions. Then the teams switch places. In most cases, it is very difficult for students to perceive taste after taste or smell after smell in a single session. We recommend one taste or one smell per team.

Empathic Considerations

Remember, your CE5 event is meant to be a positive experience. When practicing telepathic skills in combination with powerful feelings, we remind folks not to test each other by sending emotional images from negatively charged situations. *Never ever* send images of any form of injury, crisis or death during your practice just to test your receiver's abilities or see, "if they can get it."

The empaths at your event *will* perceive emotions during their practice. However, it is not acceptable (!) to try something like, "Let me see if you can tell if this person is dead." Why? Because it causes some telepaths to physically relive the death. Some natural empaths can feel that specific person's pain and suffering within their own body: physically, emotionally and spiritually! That's why!

Telepathic senders, when choosing what emotional situations you want to share, be VERY aware of whether or not your receivers have the sufficient emotional maturity to handle what you wish to emotionally project. If you have any doubts, choose another topic.

Sending and Receiving Emotions

In this exercise the sender chooses a singular emotional situation from their personal lives that they don't mind sharing with the group. The sender turns his or her back to the other students and concentrates on the memory, recalling and emotionally reliving it as much as they can. Receivers write down their perceptions: What is the sender physically feeling? What sensations - heat, cold, breeze, texture? Are they afraid? Are they joyful? Can you pick up anything of the situation?

Different Environments

Ask one person to walk out of sight of the other event participants and visit an unknown location on the property. The sender should spend 5 minutes at their chosen location. Their job is to both absorb and project everything they can about that spot. At the same time, others at your party concentrate on receiving and write down everything they can about the sender's location. What sorts of things can you try to perceive about the sender or the environment? Is the light level high or low? Is the sender hot or cold? Comfortable or uncomfortable? Inside or outside? Alone or with others? Is there movement around the sender or not? What sounds are there? What smells or tastes? In what direction is the sender relative to you? How far? Can you get a map image? Can you perceive a thread joining you and the sender? What is the sender feeling? What is he or she experiencing? Write down everything you can during the 5-minute period that the sender spends at the location. Compare notes with the sender when they return. Your sender does not necessarily have to be a group participant at your event. They can be halfway around the world. If they are absent, "introduce" the sender to the group, by showing a photo and providing a name before proceeding.

Direction and Distance

For this exercise, you need a timekeeper. This person will alert the group to certain time marks during the exercise. Choose someone known to the whole group as the sender. The sender walks away from the others and out of sight, changing course several times. After 3 minutes of walking, the sender stops. Meanwhile, back at the group, at the end of those three minutes, the timekeeper has everyone stand up and spreads out enough that they can turn a 360-degree circle to use their entire body as a telepathic receiver.

Pay attention to everything your body feels, as if each cell were a mini-antenna. Slowly turn a complete circle and first start by eliminating where the person is not. When identifying the direction of the person, look for the direction that they are in now, at this very moment. Where did they stop? Do you need to know the residual path of travel or just the end point? When you get a sense of their direction, mentally connect with the person and dowse for distance. Move your consciousness outward incrementally to find how far away they are: 100 feet/30 metres? A block? A mile/kilometre? Telepathically ask, "Are they X distance away?" Keep moving farther outward until you get a change in response or a "yes" response. Remember the old childhood games you used to play to locate a hidden object? Ask your body to respond when you are "getting warmer" or "hot" If you have telepathically gone beyond the correct distance, you may feel cooler or colder, null, or empty. Also, you are not limited to only horizontal movement. You can move upward or downward as well.

What's in a Name?

Ping another person by their name. Names have incredible power. Make sure you have the individual's full name the way they write it. Also, if they have a common name you will definitely need more detail. You don't just want to telepathically ping for just ANY John Smith on the planet. We find it easiest to use a triangulation of three different variables, such as someone's name, a personal detail about them, and their location. For example, "I'm focusing on John Smith who is wearing the green hat here at our party." You can repeat these three details in your head to move yourself into a deeper state of consciousness and send out a ping asking or calling for any information you can telepathically glean about that individual.

Telepathic Filters and Walking Connected

Practice creating your own personal safety filter telepathic bubble.

Start by sitting or lying down. Visualize or perceive yourself surrounded by a bubble that in some way filters out the energy of the rest of the world and everyone in it. If you like, make it your own personal "dome of silence." Once you can successfully both establish and hold this bubble around you then you can start to play with its "filters."

What or who do you wish to allow in? Can you successfully perceive only the individual you wish to hear and only tune in to them? Can you maintain your focus and keep out the cacophony? If you can create this telepathic connection while sitting or lying down, can you also do it when you stand up? Can you still maintain it as you walk across the room? Ping another person at the same time? Hold a conversation? Go on about your daily life all day every day?

Radio Free Universe

In the Collective Consciousness, everyone and everything from everywhere and everywhen in the Universe is broadcasting 24/7 on "Radio Free Universe."

Picture an old-fashioned radio with two knobs: one changes the channel, the other controls the volume. YOU can choose to tune into whomever and whatever you wish to listen to. Try playing with the radio dials. You don't have to listen to everything and everyone at once. You can focus on the channel or person you wish to tune into. Remember, YOU control both the volume and the station!

Map Images and Threads

You ARE connected to everything and everyone on the planet and sometimes you get a telepathic image or feel of a distant area from someone you telepathically are linking up with. Picture the connection you have with them like a bright thread between the two of you. Send an extra stream of energy to that thread to make it more obvious or visible to you. It doesn't really matter if you make the connection stand out as brilliant red, fluorescent blue, or day glow orange. Some students choose to ping another by first picturing the map or distance between them, establishing a thread (or tube), making it stronger (or bigger), and then sending their telepathic information through it.

Seeing Through the Eyes of Another

Do you have an affinity toward another species? Are you a cat person or a bird person? Do you spend a lot of time with horses? Is your best friend your dog? Can you see what or whom you are trying to locate telepathically via another's eyes? Can you perceive anything else from them telepathically via this method? If your event is located outdoors, try telepathically connecting with some of the local wildlife. Who's out there?

Walk Your Path Telepathically

Give participants a chance to try some practice holding on to their telepathic focus for longer and longer periods of time. How long can you telepathically work together without saying a word? If you already meditate while sitting, can you maintain your alpha state when you stand or while in motion? Do you perceive the live outdoor energy in a way that is different and distinct from indoor energy? What's different? How can you describe it best? Do you pick up anyone other than the other Earth Humans around you? Can you walk your path absorbing telepathic input using all of your various skills and strengths?

Working with the Elements

Outdoor telepathy practice allows you more ease in working with earth, air, fire and water elements. Each element can be used to help you move into alpha state. Have you ever telepathically listened to a bonfire? Try it. Is the crackle of the fire trying to say something? Do you ever listen to the rhythm of the falling rain? Can you catch the information stream that comes in on the wind? Is Mother Earth telling you anything?

Card Games

Ask attendees to bring a deck of cards, or have a few sets on hand. Divide the members into small groups of three or four. Each group sits down at a separate table and plays an easy game that everyone knows. Agree ahead of time that telepathic cheating is permitted and encouraged. As you play, you can practice sending and receiving. The more laughter and fun, the more success. Can you perceive a card that is about to be played? Can you ask someone telepathically to lay down a specific card? As you play, pay attention to your background thoughts as well as to what you are concentrating on in the foreground of your mind.

During the game remind everyone in your group to "tay appention" (pay attention) to ALL background fleeting thoughts when pinging to, or receiving information from, someone else. You may be asking for one sort of information but the Universe may decide to assist you by providing a little extra. You can think of it as a side note. It's like someone saying "Oh, by the way, there's also THIS additional little snippet of information." It is very common to receive more than you requested.

What About Dice or Other Kinds of Games?

Should your party goers bring things like Yahtzee or other dice tossing games? That's up to you. If anyone at your party wants to work on telekinetic energy practice, dice can be an excellent and fun means of way of testing projection skills. Energy projection work is often a side interest of our telepathy students and you get to decide if that's part of what your attendees want to focus on or give a try to.

Lots of table games can be used for telepathy practice. One of our favorites is playing "telepathic dominoes" using one set of double fifteens per group of four people. In general, we find shorter games work better than longer ones, but the game you choose simply needs to require the players to look at something and consider their options with intent before they take their turn.

APPENDIX V - MEET ET ROLE PLAY

You can discuss with your event participants what to do with your fears, or you can act out scenarios impromptu. The following exercises echo the discussion topics from Chapter 3 – What Ifs and Facing Fears.

Be a Zeta

Props needed: blank paper, marker, tape and a pair of giant costume sunglasses

Create paper signs reading "I'm from Zeta Reticuli" and "Zeta Dude with an Attitude" and have your volunteer wishing to portray ET tape it to their clothing front and back. Their instructions are to get on their knees, put on a giant pair of dark sunglasses and gesture with 4 fingers on each hand. Do not speak, but move toward people and get too close so they become uncomfortable, gesture for them to use their telepathy, whisper or blow a raspberry in their ear. How do your fellow party-goers treat this new visitor?

Equipment Failure

Props needed: Flashlights and miscellaneous electronic equipment

Role play electronic failure: Pretend all your equipment just died, the electromagnetic frequency (EMF) went off the charts and all the lights and candles extinguished at the same time. Even your flashlights won't work. Everything becomes eerily quiet, the hair on your head begins to stand straight up. How do you react? What does everyone do?

Disembodied Voices and Strange Sounds

Props needed: 2 cell phones, optional recording of strange sounds

You'll need two volunteers for this, the caller and the shill. Just before this exercise begins, out of sight of the other guests, have the caller call the shill's cell phone number. Have the shill answer the call and put their phone on its loudest speakerphone setting. While the caller mutes their own phone so nothing is accidentally broadcast, the shill rejoins the group and unobtrusively hides their phone under their chair, covered up with a piece of clothing or a hat, but still on the live call. The shill sits in their chair and makes small talk for several minutes. Caller, now you can take your phone off of its mute setting. It's your turn to have some fun. Remaining out of sight, you get to make up any voice of ET you want and say anything you would like to broadcast from the shill's hidden cell phone. You can play any strange sound you wish to play. How does everyone react? Do they investigate? How do they respond to the voice from no identifiable source?

Slightly Strange Earth Humans

Props needed: Several pieces odd or obviously out of date clothing

Pick two people out of the group and provide them with some odd and strangely out of date clothing. They may wear it in any silly way they wish. Instruct them to speak in a manner that is highly unusual. They are to use the language they normally do, but make their word choices and cadence of speech strange and hilarious. Always walking and moving side by side, as if joined at the hip, have the couple approach the other party goers and behave as if they do not know Earth customs or culture. Encourage this ET couple to come up with crazy questions only a visitor to Earth would ask. Pick up an object and examine it as if you do not know its purpose. Eat something in a way that's strange. How will attendees deal with this couple? Will they invite them to have a chair? Will someone offer them food? Will anyone remember to grab a camera?

Portals and Multi-Dimensional ETs

Props needed: Paper, marker, tape, hula hoop, costume "creature" mask, gloves

Use a hula hoop as a prop and attach a giant sign that reads, "Dimensional Portal." Provide one volunteer with a strange looking mask and gloves to role play an ET who normally resides in another dimension. Start with the hula hoop flat on the ground and have your masked ET laying on their stomach behind it. Slowly, making strange portal opening sounds, raise the hoop until it's fully upright. Have the multi-dimensional ET first stick just their hand through the portal and wave, then retract it. Then have them stick their face through, pause for a moment and retract it back to their side of the portal. Finally, ET crawls through the hoop and slowly stands up. What do your event goers do at each stage, the portal opening, the hand waving, the head peering and finally the ET emerging? How should you greet your visitor?

Missing Time

Props needed: none.

Enact a situation where one attendee suddenly rushes up to another guest obviously upset. They can't talk but are frantically tapping their wrist indicating they just had a missing time encounter. Then, a few moments later, they start speaking in strange language. Then, a half a minute after that they suddenly go silent with their mouth wide open and their eyes staring blankly! What should everyone do?

Giant Sweet and Innocent Animals

Props needed: Giant sunglasses, costume rabbit ears

We have personally witnessed extraterrestrials trying to portray themselves as animals we know well and/or ET thinks we would not be scared of such as five-foot-tall owls or four-foot-tall sharks with large black almond shaped eyes.

For this scenario, provide one person with a giant pair of sunglasses to represent dark ET eyes and costume rabbit ears. They are to put them on and go stand perfectly still like a statue, first at the edge of the group, and then a bit closer and a bit closer. If asked who they are, their first response is: "I'm a sweet little bunny rabbit from Earth just standing here, minding my own business. You believe me right?" How does the party react? Do they figure out it's a ruse? Do they offer the rabbit a seat and feed it carrots? Do they try to get the ET to remove the bunny rabbit disguise? Will your visitor comply?

Gravity Shifts

Props needed: chairs for everyone to sit in.

Sit a group of participants down in chairs and have them all pretend the gravity of the area just suddenly shifted. First, have them pretend to be nearly weightless. What do they say? How can they stay anchored and not float away? Then have the gravity suddenly become extremely heavy, preventing them from lifting even a finger to move. They're stuck. Now what? You can also add to this exercise other circumstances that the entire group might experience. What if everyone feels as if time has altered its speed? What if everyone suddenly has the hair raise up on their arms? What happens if everyone becomes frozen and the only thing they can do is talk?

Be a Sasquatch

Optional props:

- Several tree limbs stripped of leaves and side branches.
- Marbles or pebbles.
- Chair to stand on.
- Jar of stink bait.
- Star Wars™ Wookiee™ mask.

Portraying Big Brother Sasquatch gives you all kinds of options. You can walk as if you are big and huge or stand on a chair to be taller than everyone else. Your Sasquatch actor can make crashing sounds in the woods, gently toss pebbles or marbles at people's feet, roar and stomp, or bring in a bunch of long sticks and start creating a pole structure in front of them. They also need to deepen their voice as much as they can. "I'm a Sasquatch, this is MY forest. Rooaaar!!! (This can be portrayed with or without the optional costume shop Wookiee™ mask and jar of smelly stink-bait bought from your local fishing supply.) Is Big Brother alone? Are there other clan members present watching from afar? Is there another Star Nation person with them? Should you offer Brother Bigfoot a bite to eat?

Wrong Clothing

Actors needed: A man and woman willing to exchange articles of clothing.

One man and one woman are pulled aside together, out of sight of the other participants. They agree to exchange and wear articles of each other's clothing in a strange or silly fashion. They get to choose what it is and how they wear it incorrectly, be it backwards, inside out, on their head, over top of their own clothing, etc. Make it obvious, highly unusual and as hilarious as you can. The couple finishes trading attire and are instructed as to how to act and what to say when they rejoin the group. Have the couple return to rest of the group as if nothing is wrong and act as if they are unaware of their strange clothing malfunctions. When it's finally pointed out to them, the couple suddenly realize they are wearing someone else's clothing oddly and each say out loud something like, "Hey this isn't my shirt. Why am I wearing this? It's on backwards! Whose shirt is this? What's going on here?!" How do the rest of your fellow contactees react? Do they only laugh or does someone figure out the couple might just have had a close encounter of the trippy kind?

Be an Invisible ET

Props needed: 4 sheets of blank paper, marker, tape, large moveable mirror or several small hand mirrors. Optional full spectrum camera.

Introduce the idea to your attendees that some of your Star Nation visitors may show up but maintain invisibility as their mission protocol. Tell them that if they spot the tell-tale signs of an invisible person walking among you to let everyone else know you may have a visitor. All your participants must understand that invisible people cannot be easily seen by looking directly at them. They can sometimes be spotted more easily using peripheral vision, angled reflection, or a full spectrum camera.

Next you need two volunteers willing to be invisible ETs. Make 4 paper signs that say in large print, "I'M INVISIBLE" and "YOU CAN'T SEE ME." (You can get clever and add fun comments like, "Nothing to see here" or "I'm just a shimmer of my former self.") Tape these signs to the front and back of your volunteers. They are to wander around, inspect people in the group, pick up objects (that appear to float in mid-air with no support) or simply mess with whatever and whoever they want in an amusing way. How does the group respond to an invisible ET in their midst? What do they say to your ET guest? Does anyone think to instruct your visitor where to stand so they can be seen in a mirror? Do they offer them anything? What happens next? (You can also use the "I'M INVISIBLE" paper signs in on Big Brother in the *Being Sasquatch* exercise as well.)

You can have all kinds of fun with this type of "Meet ET" role playing. Use your imagination. Putting attendees through exercises like these has proven to be extremely helpful in getting your CE5 party guests to not only think through what they would do and say in various possible scenarios, but they get to act it out as well.

Tlkm (Sandia)

Commander of the Sandia Mountain P'nti Facility
on the eastern edge of Albuquerque, New Mexico (USA).

Jrooti
Communications specialist and cultural liaison.

R'hz (Radar)
Pilot, stellar cartographer and Earth media specialist.

T'ni (Teenie)
Telepathy instructor and Official First Contact facilitator.

P'ta or Pita
Official First Contact Cultural liaison trainee.

Gst or Grayson
Official First Contact Cultural liaison trainee.

GLOSSARY

Abalone shell - shell of the marine species Haliotis midae. A 4" – 6" (10 – 15 cm) diameter abalone half shell is often used as a bowl for burning sage.

Abductee (see Experiencer)

Adrenaline - hormone produced by the adrenal glands that prompts fight or flight response.

Alpha - slower brain wave state associated with meditation and increased telepathic reception.

Amygdala - almond shaped structures which are part of the brain's hippocampus that are involved in emotions and the reception of emotional carrier wave telepathy runs on.

Appention, tay (see Tay appention)

Auditory telepaths - telepaths who easily send and receive via sound and vibration.

Aura - energy field generated by the body.

Blink blink - unofficial phrase used which refers to telepathically asking an ET pilot telepathically to double blink their vessel's lights.

Bowl, offering the (see Offering the Bowl)

Camouflage, cloud (see Cloud Camouflage)

Close Encounter of the First Kind (CE1) - I saw a light in the sky: You have a visual sighting of an unidentified flying object.

Close Encounter of the Second Kind (CE2) - something affected a person or the environment: A UFO event where a physical effect is alleged: electronic or vehicle malfunction, animals reacting, physical paralysis, physical traces on the ground affecting nearby plants, a chemical or radiation trace, etc.

Close Encounter of the Third Kind (CE3) - I saw a person or a being: UFO encounters in which an animated creature is present whether its humanoid, robot, and humans or other beings who are associated with a vehicle.

Close Encounter of the Fourth Kind (CE4) - something trippy happens and your sense of reality is transformed in some way. This includes absurd, hallucinatory or dreamlike events.

Close Encounter of the Fifth Kind (CE5) - voluntary back and forth communication with a Star Nation person. A UFO event that involves voluntary direct communication between Star Nation people and Earth humans. You talk back and forth to each other.

Cloud camouflage - a cloaking or masking of an extraterrestrial craft using artificially generated cloud vapor.

Clouds, hello the (see Hello the Clouds)

Collective Consciousness - the concept that all information, from everything and everyone from everywhere and every when is connected together in the unseen world.

Consciousness, collective (see Collective consciousness)

Contact, official first (see Official First Contact)

Dimensional Nations - sentient beings who do not normally reside in a physical body but who can, by their own choice, take physical form.

Electromagnetic frequency (EMF) - a physical field produced by electrically charged objects that affects the behavior of other things within the vicinity. The field can be viewed as a combination of an electric field as well as a magnetic one.

Elementals - conscious sentient beings who exist in the elements earth, air, fire and water.

EMF (see Electromagnetic frequency)

Emotional overwhelm - emotional extreme brought on by a sudden emotional, physical or spiritual shock.

Empaths - telepaths who easily perceive emotional energy from a person, place or thing.

ET (see Extraterrestrial)

Experiencer - individual who has experienced an event involving a UFO or extraterrestrial. Synonymous with the word contactee.

Extraterrestrial - any individual who does not call this planet their birth place of origin.

Fight or flight response - common phrase used for a sudden surge of adrenaline.

Find your tribe - phrase that encourages CE5 participants to seek out other like-minded people who accept and understand them for who they are.

First contact (see Official First Contact)

Full spectrum camera - specialized cameras capable of recording in a broad light spectrum that goes beyond Earth Human sight limitations, from ultraviolet to infrared light.

Gesture for missing time - urgently tapping with two fingers of one hand on the back of the wrist of the opposite hand where wrist watches are normally worn is the gesture for "I just experienced missing time."

Global Positioning System or GPS - satellite-based radionavigation system used to provide latitude and longitude coordinates.

Goosebumps - (alternatively goose pimples or goose flesh) a skin response that raises the hairs on your body.

GPS (see Global Positioning System)

Grey - common derogatory catch-all term for any hairless, large headed, bipedal, short statured extraterrestrial possessing big dark eyes.

Grounding and Centering (see Appendix III)

Hello the Clouds - standard phrasing used for a telepathic greeting to the local skyspace searching for anyone who might happen to be in the vicinity listening.

Kinesthetic telepaths - individuals whose innate telepathic skill set includes perception via touch.

Missing time - common phrase used by experiencers of extraterrestrial contact that indicates they have parts of their memory that are incomplete.

Missing time, gesture for (see Gesture for Missing Time)

Multi-dimensional Nations - sentient beings who have either the innate or mechanical ability to step from one dimensional time/space to another.

OFC (see Official First Contact)

Offering the Bowl - the universal gesture of forming hands together to make a bowl which translates as "gift" or "I have something for you."

Official First Contact (OFC) - phrase used by the P'nti for the upcoming official public meeting of Earth Human representatives with Star Nation representatives.

Orbs - general catch all term used for any ball of light which seems to be able to move under its own power and have an intelligence.

Overwhelm, emotional (see Emotional overwhelm)

Peripheral vision - what you see at the very side edges of your vision if your eyes are looking straight ahead.

Plasma - a state of matter in which some or all of the electrons have been torn from their parent atoms and where the negatively charged electrons and positively charged ions move independently. Plasmas are often associated with very high temperatures. Much of our sun is a plasma.

Pleiadian worlds - generally referring to any of several inhabited worlds in the Pleiades constellation area of our Milky Way galaxy.

Pineal gland - a pea-sized conical mass of tissue in the brain, secreting a hormonelike substance in some mammals, thought to also be involved in telepathic reception.

Ping - common term used for a telepathic hello sent or received.

P'nti - referring to anyone from the planet P'ntl.

P'ntl - the fifth planet orbiting Zeta Reticuli II.

Portal - a general term that means doorway, entry or exit point. "What looked like a dimensional portal open up right in front of the ship."

Radio Free Universe - phrase given to the concept that the Collective Consciousness is broadcasting information from everything and everyone from everywhere and every when all the time.

Realm, unseen (see Unseen realm)

Receivers - general term for anyone who is doing the telepathic receiving.

Reticulum - a Southern Hemisphere constellation whose name means small net.

Rightminded - unselfish thoughts and actions that consider the long-term sustainable balance physically, emotionally and spiritually.

Sage, white (see White sage)

Senders - general term for anyone who is doing the telepathic sending.

Sasquatch - North American term for any bipedal, large, hairy forest dweller. Also, commonly called Big Brother or Bigfoot.

Shill - slang term for someone who's in on the act or the ruse.

Skipper ships - classic saucers shaped vessels designed primarily for short travel within a single solar system, used for planetary missions of up to 6 crew members.

Smudge - (noun) smoke from dried white sage leaves used to clear away negative energy. Smudge can also refer to the dried leaves themselves as in, "Did you bring the smudge?" instead of, "Did you bring the white sage?" (verb) the act of using the smoke of white sage to clear away negative energy from a person or a space. See Appendix I.

Smudge stick - a bundle of white sage leaves bound together with cotton thread or twine. Smudge sticks can have other herbs such as sweetgrass, cedar, lavender, etc. mixed in with them, but the main necessary component is the white sage.

Smudging station - a location where sage, fire and a container are available for folks to smudge themselves off anytime they feel the need. Ours are very simple and consist of a purchased smudge stick, a hand held lighter, and an empty large metal can with a sign.

Spatial telepaths - folks who naturally both send and receive better telepathically when they are in motion and who often innately possess a unique blend of visual, auditory, and kinesthetic skill.

Star Nation - polite term used to refer to anyone who doesn't call this planet home. Other acceptable terms include: extraterrestrials, visitors, ETs and interstellar family.

Tay appention - a word play on the phrase "pay attention," specifically twisted to get people to think a second time. "Tay appention there's gonna be a test." (Rev. White Otter)

__Telepathy 101 Primer__ - basic "How-to" guide dictated to and written in collaboration with a P'nti woman by the name of T'ni from the Sandia Mountain Station east of Albuquerque, New Mexico, USA.

Tribe, find your (see Find Your Tribe)

Unseen realm - beings and things that are beyond what your eyes can see.

Vision, peripheral (see Peripheral vision)

Visual telepaths - people who naturally pick up telepathic information via images.

White sage - native herb whose dried leaves are burned and the smoke used in an incense like fashion along with prayer to remove negative energy and clear a person or a space.

Woodben - any sentient being who lives in the woods anywhere on Earth. No matter their size, if the forest is their home, they are part of the woodben.

Wrongminded - selfish thoughts and actions that do not consider the long term sustainable balance physically, emotionally and spiritually.

Zetas - slang term often incorrectly used to describe several similar looking Star Nations who have large heads, no obvious hair, four fingers on each hand and large eyes, often covered with dark lenses.

Zeta Reticuli II - the further of the two stars that make up the binary system of Zeta Reticuli in the Southern Hemisphere constellation of Reticulum, approximately 40 light years from Earth.

Biographies

Su Walker

As a professional clairvoyant and medical intuitive for nearly thirty years, Su Walker has been featured on both national and international television. Su is also a lifelong experiencer of ET/UFO phenomena. In September 2013, she was unexpectedly contacted by an extraterrestrial while visiting the Albuquerque, New Mexico area for the first time. A strong friendship with this ET, nicknamed Sandia, began to develop with she and her spouse, Rev. White Otter. For the past five years, this couple has continued to dialogue with and translate for not only Sandia (Commander Tlkm) but also several other extraterrestrials who operate out of a facility beneath the Sandia Mountain. Since June 2015, together Su and Otter have volunteered more than 10,000 hours assisting in telepathic translation for the Twitter account @sandiawisdom. They have aided in translating the first known collaborative Earth Human/P'nti publication. A basic training manual entitled *The Telepathy 101 Primer* available as a free download from officialfirstcontact.com, and coming soon in hard copy. For more information visit www.suwalker.com.

Rev. White Otter

White Otter has traveled the shaman's path for more than four decades and has been involved with teaching energy work for most of that time. A true Renaissance man, Otter holds a masters in philosophy and a degree in the culinary arts. He has been a professional French chef and a nurseryman as well as a historic 18th century reenactor. Amongst other things, he tells us he has spent 35 years studying, "... the energetic parallels of the multi-dimensional world that we live in." Otter has been a lifelong contactee and has spent the last 5 years working with wife Su Walker as a telepathic translator for the P'nti of the Sandia Mountain complex. When asked where he's from, Otter will only reply, "I'm not from here."

Made in the USA
Columbia, SC
30 December 2021